THE LIBRARY OF
CONTEMPORARY THOUGHT

*America's most original voices
tackle today's most provocative issues*

ROBERT HUGHES

A JERK ON ONE END
Reflections of a Mediocre Fisherman

"The last time I passed a weekend pursuing tarpon in the Florida Keys, there were the air tickets to Miami and back, the car rental, the motel in Islamorada with its corroded faucets and the sexual galumphing coming from the other side of the thin wall, the boat charter and guiding costs: all, in the end, for one brief connection with one large silver fish, which made two reel-burning runs, treated me to a frenzied display of clattering, shining leaps, spat out the fly, and vanished. And yet it would be contemptible to complain. Fishing largely consists of not catching fish; failure is as much a part of the sport as knee injuries are of football."

A Jerk on One End

Reflections of a Mediocre Fisherman

Robert Hughes

The Library of Contemporary Thought
The Ballantine Publishing Group • New York

The Library of Contemporary Thought
Published by The Ballantine Publishing Group

Copyright © 1999 by Robert Hughes

Grateful acknowledgment is made to the following for
permission to reprint previously published material:

HarperCollins Publishers (Australia) Pty Ltd.: Excerpt from
"Captain Dobbin" from *Collected Poems* by Kenneth Slessor,
Angus & Robertson Ltd., 1994.

Alfred A. Knopf, Inc., and the Arthur Waley Estate: Excerpt from
"Fishing in the Wei River" by Po Chu-I from *Translations from
the Chinese,* translated by Arthur Waley, published in the U.S. by
Alfred A. Knopf, Inc., and in Great Britain by Allen & Unwin in
1946 and Unwin Paperbacks in 1982 as *Chinese Poems.* Copyright
© 1947 and renewed 1969 by Alfred A. Knopf, Inc. Reprinted by
permission of Alfred A. Knopf, Inc., and the Arthur Waley Estate.

http://www.randomhouse.com/BB/

LIBRARY OF CONGRESS CATALOGING-IN-PUBLICATION DATA
Hughes, Robert, 1938–
A jerk on one end : reflections of a mediocre fisherman / Robert
Hughes.—1st ed.
    p.   cm.—(The Library of contemporary thought)
        ISBN 0-345-42283-X (hc. : alk. paper)
            1. Fishing. I. Title. II. Series.
                SH443.H768   1999
799.1—dc21   99-21234
                                                         CIP

Text design by Holly Johnson

Manufactured in the United States of America

First Edition: October 1999

10   9   8   7   6   5   4   3   2   1

To Doris

There was a young lady of Wales,
Who caught a large fish without scales;
When she lifted the hook
She exclaimed: "Only look!"
That extatic young lady of Wales.

—EDWARD LEAR, IN

A BOOK OF NONSENSE (1846)

Acknowledgments

Over the years I have fished with many people and learned something from them all. But I particularly want to set down my debt and gratitude to four of them. In alphabetical order, then: To John Alexander, the Texas Terror. To Peter Duchin, companion and best of friends on many a fly-fishing excursion to Alaska and to northen Quebec. To Henry Kravis, who for the past few years in Colorado has shown me a level of trout fishing (and of hospitality) whose existence I had scarcely even imagined. And to Alan Shields, skipper of *Stinkpot IV,* for getting me back into sea fishing after I moved to Long Island.

The quotations from Po Chu-I's *Fishing in*

the Wei River, John Donne's *Sermon on Matthew 4:18–20,* and James Saunders's *The Compleat Fisherman* are taken from that excellent compendium *The Magic Wheel: An Anthology of Fishing in Literature,* edited by David Profumo and Graham Smith (1985).

I

SALT WATER

"A JERK ON ONE END OF a line, waiting for a jerk on the other." Such is one of the classic folk definitions of fishing. It echoes Samuel Johnson's description of the sport as a stick and a string, with a worm on one end and a fool on the other. And who can doubt its truth? In some ways it's a ridiculous human passion. I keep a fishing boat on Shelter Island, where I live. It is an open, center-console twenty-five-foot Mako, built in 1979. It cost $12,000 when I bought it, second-hand, in 1981. Every year it costs me about $4,000 in dockage charges (six months of the year) and haulage and storage (the other six). I am not mechanically minded, and what lies under the cowling of its now aging 1988 Evinrude 225 is as complete a mystery to me as the meaning of the inscriptions on a Mayan stela. If it broke down at sea, I would be utterly at a loss. Its maintenance I leave to the experts at the boatyard, who charge about $50 an hour for the work. It drinks gas at the rate of about two miles to the gallon, and has a complicated oil-mixture system with an alarm beeper hooked into it. Of late, this beeper has taken to going off—a shrill, moronic warble that stops as mysteriously as it starts—when the engine seems to be running perfectly, nothing discernible is wrong, and the oil tank is more than half full, usually on a hard-running tide in the strait between Orient Point and Plum Gut or, even worse, in the big rip known as the Race off Fishers Island, twenty miles from home, thus filling me with a sense of incompetence and dread at the prospect of drifting helplessly off into the deep Atlantic. This diminishes the feeling of oceanic peace and oneness with the cosmos that the more mystical-minded fishing writers claim to be the reward of their sport. All in all, were I to amortize the market value of the fish I catch in a year against the expense of catching them, I would say I was spending about $55 per pound on bluefish, which, scaled and filleted, can be had in the local store for about $3.99.

And this doesn't include what other kinds of fishing cost. The last time I passed a weekend pursuing tarpon in the Florida Keys, for instance, there were the air tickets to Miami and back, the car rental, the motel in Islamorada with its corroded faucets and the sexual galumphing coming from the other side of the thin wall, the boat charter and guiding costs: all, in the end, for one brief connection with one large silver fish, which made two reel-burning runs, treated me to a frenzied display of clattering, shining leaps, spat out the fly, and vanished. And yet it would be contemptible to complain. Fishing largely consists of not catching fish; failure is as much a part of the sport as knee injuries are of football.

I have fished a good deal of my life. Not professionally, of course, and not with enough dedication to qualify as "expert," however you might define that. But constantly enough, and with sufficient enthusiasm, to call myself an addict. I grew up on Sydney Harbor, in Australia. In the late 1940s and early 1950s its waters had plenty of fish in them. (Today they do again; it was during the 1960s and 1970s that the harbor waters became so polluted that most of the fish vanished, their spawn poisoned by industrial effluents. They have since made a comeback.) Mostly I would fish with a hand line from a pier that stuck out into Rose Bay at the bottom of Cranbrook Road, where our house was. One could always see small fish—mainly yellowtail, a species of jack—swimming in the clear green water around its worn and splintery pilings. One would take a pellet of stale bread, wet it with spit, and mold it around a tiny hook tied to a fine monofilament line with no sinker. The white scrap would sink slowly, slowly in the water. The trick was to take up as much slack as possible without lifting the bait up. With luck, one of the little jacks would charge it and there would be the electric jolt of contact with a creature utterly unlike oneself, which would then be pulled in, its silver body frantically quivering. On the bottom, with a sinker, one could also catch leatherjackets—a small and rather torpid triggerfish, named for the toughness of its hide—and the occasional red bream, the baby version of the giant red snapper that inhabited deeper waters, off the harbor's headlands. Since my mother generally refused to cook these small victims, they were given to the cat or ended up in the garbage. Only once did I catch anything resembling a game fish, when by the sheerest fluke a small passing bonito grabbed my bait just as it hit the water. It couldn't have weighed more than five or six pounds, but I still have the faint white scars on my index finger left by the hand line. Fifty years later they have faded to near invisibility, but I can still see them. I couldn't have been more pleased if they had been dueling scars. Sucking my cuts, admiring the dying fish as its colors faded on the dock, surrounded by a ring of awed kids my own age, I felt the first surge of triumph in my life.

I had never felt this sense of prowess from any other sport: I was neither good nor bad at athletics, just skinny, unmotivated, and fast in spurts, and I rather disliked team games, especially rugby, at which I was hopelessly bad. My idea of a contact sport was chess. Among the kids at school I had the largely deserved reputation of being an intellectual snob and a smart-ass. Guilty as charged. Fishing enabled me to be alone; to dream, yet with the senses on full alert. It saved me, to some degree, from the guilt of not fitting in with the peculiarly intense collectivity of boarding school. Nobody was watching.

Other sports made my failures conspicuous: the cricket ball scooped into the air, an easy catch for the hostile fielder; my humiliating fumble of the baton in a relay race. But you did not fail at fishing, even if you caught nothing; you just "had a bad day" because the fish didn't cooperate. Years later, in the late sixties, while reading Leonardo da Vinci's notebooks to prepare for a book that I wound up never writing, I came across this sentence: *"Se sei solo sarai tutto tuo"*—if you are alone, you are entirely your own man. Fishing is, or should be, a thoughtful business. I was often told that rugby players think, but on the field I couldn't—I was too consumed with terror that if the greasy rugby ball ever reached me on the wing, the phalanx of giant country boys from western New South Wales would bear down on me with their knobbly knees, fixing to mash me into the mud.

I cannot think of a single benefit I received from having to play rugby, beyond a thin veneer of stoicism produced not by genuine courage but by the fear of being thought a wimp. But there were several ways in which fishing formed my imagination as a child. It taught me something of the craft of handling time; it helped me overcome the inbuilt impatience of childhood, and I was an impatient kid who wanted quick results, fast tracks from desire to its satisfaction.

You cannot hurry fishing, because it is the fish, not you, that decides the tempo. This continuous absorptive contact with the harbor turned me toward the literature of the sea. Most Australian schoolkids of my generation were taught to memorize a poem of John Masefield's that began, "I must go down to the sea again, to the lonely sea and the sky," but on digging a collected Masefield out of my father's library, I was enthralled by *Dauber,* his long narrative poem—largely autobiographical, though I didn't realize that at the time—about a boy who wants to be a painter but runs away to sea on a four-master bound across the Atlantic to Cape Horn, where he meets his death. I read *Lord Jim,* and Joshua Slocum's memoirs of his solitary voyage around the world in the little sloop *Spray*; and, best of all for its direct appeal to a thirteen-year-old boy, Rudyard Kipling's wonderful bildungsroman of another thirteen-year-old's passage to early manhood through the rough comradeship of a Grand Banks schooner's crew, *Captains Courageous.* There were even poems about Sydney Harbor itself, which strongly affected me: Kenneth Slessor's *Five Bells,* his great elegy for a bohemian friend who drowned after falling overboard from a Manly ferry with his pockets full of beer bottles—the Australian *Lycidas,* as someone called it; and, hardly less suggestive, his evocation of a retired Pacific mariner, *Captain Dobbin,* living out his last years in a brick villa by the harbor and logging the comings and goings of its sea traffic:

For at night, when the stars mock
 themselves with lanterns,
So late the chimes blow loud and faint
Like a hand shutting and unshutting over
 the bells,
Captain Dobbin, having observed from bed
The lights, like a great fiery snake, of the
 Comorin
Going to sea, will note the hour
For subsequent recording in his gazette.

But the sea is really closer to him than this,
Closer to him than a dead, lovely woman,
For he keeps bits of it, like old letters,
Salt tied up in bundles,
Or pressed flat,
What you might call a lock of the sea's hair,
So Captain Dobbin keeps his dwarfed
 memento,
His urn-burial, a chest of mummied waves,
Gales fixed in print, and the sweet
 dangerous countries
Of shark and casuarina-tree,
Stolen and put in colored maps,
Like a flask of sea-water, or a bottled ship,
A schooner caught in a glass bottle;
But Captain Dobbin keeps them in books . . .

So nightly he sails from shelf to shelf,
Or to the quadrants, dangling with rusty
    screws,
Or the hanging-gardens of old charts,
So old they bear the authentic protractor-
    lines,
Traced in faint ink, as fine as Chinese hairs.

Over the flat and painted atlas-leaves
His reading-glass would tremble,
Over the fathoms, pricked in tiny rows,
Water shelving to the coast.
Quietly the bone-rimmed lens would float
Till, through the glass, he felt the barbed rush
Of bubbles foaming, spied the albacores,
The blue-finned admirals . . .

I longed to see those albacores, those blue-
finned admirals. And I can never see an old brass-
bound quadrant in a junk store without thinking
of Captain Dobbin and his author. Under such in-
fluences, the Pacific opened to my boy's imagination as a sort of epic space, charted by others but
not experienced by me, and I yearned to know it.
This longing has never been satisfied, and now
that I am sixty, I do not expect it to be. My family
had no boat, no maritime background. My father

had been a flier—one of the pioneers who flew their Sopwith Camels and Bristol Fighters against the Germans in World War I—but he couldn't have been less interested in boating, or any kind of saltwater fishing. So I rarely got out of the harbor and was confined to its foreshores, rocks, and piers. No matter; though I didn't really know it at the time, I was getting an education in seeing and discriminating. To fish at all, even on a humble level, you must notice things: the movement of the water and its patterns, the rocks, the seaweed, the quiver of tiny scattering fish that betrays a bigger predator under them. Time on the pier taught me to concentrate on the visual, for fishing is intensely visual even—perhaps especially—when nothing is happening. It is easy to look, but learning to *see* is a more gradual business, and it sneaks up on you unconsciously, by stealth. The sign that it is happening is the fact that you are not bored by the absence of the spectacular. And the harbor had its own character. It was not an Arcadian bay, but a big, variegated industrial port, full of heavy-duty maritime structures as well as small sandy coves and virgin headlands of tumbled rocks. I came to love the straightforward, functional shapes of old rust-streaked hulls and pylons, buoys and bollards, wooden posts and docks. These demotic forms intrigued me as the genteel artifacts of upper-middle-class Australian life, the "good" furniture and the silverware produced on special occasions, did not; they had a strength that went beyond questions of taste, and ever since, I have delighted in vernacular, practical objects, things made straightforwardly for use in work. Nothing about them was superfluous. Each had a history of use, which I liked to ponder and even fantasize about: the decaying hull half sunk in the sand of Rose Bay beach, the mysterious, rusting, rivet-bound cylinder that might have been a buoy or a steam boiler. "Objects gross and the unseen soul are one," wrote Walt Whitman in "A Song for Occupations" (1881), his paean to American craft and making.

I also became aware of a kind of fishing that was entirely beyond me, and to which I hardly dared aspire. Big-game fishing in Australia was in its raw beginnings fifty years ago. It required boats and tackle that were so specialized, so difficult to come by, and so costly as to be beyond the reach of most Australians. But the waters of Sydney—both inside the harbor and outside in the Pacific—held an abundance of sharks, and these possessed an iconic status in Australian imagination, because they were our only big carnivores, the only creatures that posed a threat to human life. The land had its dangerous reptiles and insects, but nothing that walked, slithered, or flew was going to actually gobble you up, except for the saltwater crocodile, *Crocodylus porosus,* whose habitat lay thousands of miles away in the tropical north. In the sea, however, it was different. There one might find the great white, the mako, the tiger, the gray nurse, the hammerhead—or, possibly, they might find you. Since the population of Sydney was largely amphibious, and liked then as now to go swimming during its lunch hour, the man-eater loomed large in civic imagination—though in practice it ate few men (or women or children), it was always *there*, a trigger of latent fear. The beaches inside the harbor were ringed with shark-proof nets or enclosed with iron mesh; on the ocean beaches, vigilant lifeguards scanned the surf from wooden towers, looking for the distant black chip of a fin cutting the water. There were a few laconic heroes who specialized in catching sharks with thick hand lines from rowboats; one of them, in defiance of all caution, did so from the rocks at Bondi Beach and killed scores of them over the years. But only people who lived at Bondi were likely to witness these struggles; I never did. The one place where you could actually see the finny criminal close up was the wharf station at Watson's

Bay, just inside the arm of South Head, where the Sydney big-game fishing club strung up its catches to weigh them on a steelyard.

When a big shark was towed in behind a boat, it was the nearest thing to a public hanging. The word would begin to spread as soon as the fishermen docked. The nearby pub and the fish-and-chip shops would empty. Before the shark was even halfway out of the water a crowd would have assembled to see the malefactor receive his final humiliation. Two hundred or three hundred was a common number: pink sunburned fathers squinting in the afternoon light, mums in floral print dresses, kids spooning Peter's ice cream out of paper cups. A family spectacle, like Tyburn in the 1780s. Sometimes the shark would still be alive, and it was the vitality that fascinated me. Eight hundred pounds of fish, twelve feet long, had been dragged thrashing to a standstill miles out in the Pacific. They had gaffed it and got a tailrope on it. Then, commonly, it had been shot several times in the head with a heavy rifle or a rusty shotgun loaded with ball, to quiet it down. Then they had towed it by the tail, the water sluicing backward through its gill slots—enough to drown any fish, you'd think—with its blood running in a dilute stream in the wake, sharp dark crimson fading out to a faint pink, all those miles back to the dock. As the tailrope was hooked to the lifting chain and the winch began to clatter, the oldies on the wharf would produce their laconic yarns of dread for the twelve-year-olds. *You should never haul a big shark into the boat if you have any choice about it. You think he's dead, but he's not. He's just playing possum. He'll bite your weewee off faster than you can say Joe Stalin, sonny, and take your arse with it as well. Me mate Jack, he had his back broken by a mako when it woke up in the cockpit. Three months in Saint Vincent's. You can't fool with the bastards. Better stand back.*

And we did. As the shark rose out of the water I would be frozen by a delicious terror that, I would learn from Edmund Burke a decade later, is the root of the sublime. Ugly as sin, with its stomach protruding from its jaws, pressed out by vertical gravity: and yet as beautiful as Lucifer in its completeness—a mighty eating machine. Quite often it would be still alive. It would give one contorted thrash and bite the wharf, sometimes leaving a tooth or two in the iron-hard timber: the criminal uttering a last curse from the scaffold. After hanging for a while, with its weight and the boat's name chalked on its now dry flank, it would be let down, dragged through the water to the beach in front of what is now Doyle's Seafood Restaurant, and cut up, just as Georgian murderers had been delivered to the anatomizing surgeons. Its meat went for fertilizer, probably: nobody in Sydney wanted to eat an old shark, though smaller ones were sold in fish markets under the euphemistic name of "flake." Sometimes, even then, the shark didn't seem to know it was dead. I once saw the heart cut out of a big mako: a shiny pink lobe of muscle, a foot and a half long. It continued to convulse and beat on the beach for twenty minutes after it was separated from the body, as though it were trying to get back down the sand into the water. So much for those comic strips in which Dick Daring finished off a shark underwater with a well-placed stab of his knife. You might as well take on a tank with a teaspoon.

Without reducing my enthusiasm for fishing, such gory sights had, I now realize, a permanent effect on me. They increased the fascination the sea had for me—that mysterious, wild world below the surface, filled with only superficially familiar creatures whose existence was so utterly remote from that of human beings. The fundamental experience of fishing consists of dropping a line into the unknown. You can guess at what is down there; you can make your best estimates based on tide, habitat, feeding patterns, and so forth; but you do not really know. Whatever takes your hook therefore has a character of revelation, even if it's only a flounder. It may be edible or not; thorny, spiny, or beautifully sleek; equipped with gnashing jaws or relatively passive; but there is always, assuming that you aren't sight-fishing, the magic moment when the thing struggling on your line down there could be *anything*. The similarities between the writer's work and the angler's need not be labored, but they exist: The writer lets down his or her hook into the deposit of memory and experience, the semiconscious fluid—not the dark, abyssal unconscious, which is out of reach, but the tidal zone where word, phrase, idea, and memory circulate in a kind of half-light, forming their unpredicted patterns. With luck, you bring something up. If it is undersize, you toss it back.

In earlier times, the inscrutability of the sea bred fantasy. The water's surface was the limit of the rational world. Below it, before the age of hydrography, ichthyology, and the Aqua-Lung, was the abode of demons, monsters, and every sort of blood-freezing deformity: a zone without limits in which imagination could run free. The biblical archetype of these sea beasts was Leviathan. By the sixteenth century they had bred and mutated

without limits, and were to the Mannerist imagination what space aliens are to us. Here is Edmund
Spenser, in Canto XII of *The Faerie Queen*, listing
the horrors his sea voyagers confront after their
passage between quicksand and whirlpool:

> an hideous hoast arrayd
> Of huge Sea Monsters, such as living sense
>   dismayd.

> Most ugly shapes, and horrible aspects,
> Such as Dame Nature selfe mote [might]
>   feare to see,
> Or shame, that ever should so fowle defects
> From her most cunning hand escaped be;
> All dreadful pourtraicts of deformitee:
> Spring-headed *Hydraes*, and sea-shouldring
>   Whales,
> Great whirlpools, which all fishes make to
>   flee,
> Bright Scolopendraes, arm'd with silver scales,
> Mighty *Monoceros*, with immeasured tayles.

> The dreadfull Fish, that hath deserv'd the
>   name
> Of Death, and like him lookes in dreadfull
>   hew,

The griesly Wasserman, that makes his game
The flying ships with swiftnesse to pursew,
The horrible Sea-Satyre, that doth shew
His fearefull face in time of greatest storme,
Huge *Ziffius*, whom Mariners eschew
No less than rocks (as travellers informe)
And greedy *Rosmarines* with visages deforme.

All these, and thousand thousands many more,
And more deformed Monsters thousand fold,
With dreadfull noise, and hollow rombling
    rore,
Came rushing in the fomy waves enrold,
Which seem'd to fly for fear, them to behold:
No wonder, if these did the knight appall;
For all that here on earth we dreadful hold,
Be but as bugs to fearen babes withall,
Compared to creatures in the seas entrall
    [entrails, inner parts].

Hydras were giant squid; "huge *Ziffius*" was the swordfish, *Xiphias gladius* (the Greek and Latin words for "sword" conjoined), which had a reputation for driving its bill into the hulls of boats; but who knows what a grisly Wasserman or a greedy Rosmarine might have been? (Methinks I see them on a Manhattan office directory: Rosmarine and

Wasserman, divorce attorneys.) Sea creatures mutated into wonders in the minds of those who had never seen one. The classic example is the mermaid, who is often said (by those seeking rational explanations of irrational fears and desires) to have originated with the manatee or dugong, though a sailor would need to be either very shortsighted or quite deranged with randiness to mistake one of these fat mammals for a tempting water nymph. People had been seeing and catching dolphin all over the waters of the world by the eighteenth century, and yet the standard dolphin of the visual arts bore no relation to the real, sleek, graceful creature that followed ships, which artists, as Benjamin Franklin complained in his shipboard diary of an Atlantic passage in 1726, had "improved into a crooked monster with a head and eyes like a bull, a hog's snout, and a tail like a blown tulip."

Today, these mythological forms of marine otherness are fading from the culture—though they have not entirely gone. They reappear in the images of creatures that practically none of us are going to see except in photographs—the phosphorescent, hair-tailed weirdnesses of the abyssal depths, the barely studied fauna that cluster around boiling volcanic clefts on the ocean floor, the living fossil of a coelacanth dragged by the merest fluke from deep water and paraded on a wheelbarrow through an Indonesian port market. Thanks to them, the sea remains in some ways richer in anomalies than the Middle Ages or the Renaissance ever imagined. It is a somewhat abstract, conceptual strangeness, since the ordinary fisherman has no contact with such beings.

In America a century ago, it was otherwise. Not only were American fisheries amazingly abundant, but they held forms of marine life that no sport fisherman had ever dared attack before. The possibility of heroic, almost mythic, encounter was still there, latent in American nature. Henry Longfellow presumably sensed this when he had his Indian hero Hiawatha go after the sturgeon Nahma, "king of fishes," all alone in a birch canoe with a line of twisted cedar bark; Nahma, as though in a rehearsal for *Jaws*, is provoked into leaping upward from the depths and swallowing both Hiawatha and his canoe. (As a matter of record, sturgeon can't swallow people, let alone boats, not that it mattered to Longfellow.) From the 1890s on, a new and particularly American genre of fishing writing came into its own: fishing as dangerous safari, in pursuit of enormous prey. The surface of the sea—Nova Scotia in the north, but especially the waters of Florida and the islands and reefs of the Caribbean—became a watery veldt traversed by wild giants such as the various billfish (black marlin, blue marlin, striped marlin, broadbill swordfish), the shark (not something you deliberately fished for at first, but were bound to contend with), the giant bluefin tuna, and the tarpon. In part, the pursuit of these creatures was made possible by technical advances in tackle—stronger rods, more capacious reels, tougher line. But it also came out of a peculiar kind of will that had nothing to do with the older, more contemplative ideals of angling. There is a manic quality to some of the late-nineteenth-century writing about saltwater fishing, produced by "great white hunters" such as Charles Frederick Holder (1851–1915): Anything that swims, no matter how harmless or inedible, becomes an object of obsessive pursuit merely because it is big and unfamiliar. If you read Holder in *Big Game at Sea* (1908) on hunting a manta ray to death, for instance, hurling lance after lance into the enormous beast until, weakened and disoriented, it bleeds to death in the shallows off the Florida coast, you are struck by two main features of his narrative: first, the undeniable pluck and tenacity it must have taken to attempt such a hunt, but second, the utter pointlessness of the whole exercise.

The early high-water mark of American

big-game fishing came in the 1930s, when a small group of mainly American enthusiasts—the equivalents of the African hunting guides of the late nineteenth century—shaped the sport to the point where, in 1940, Michael Lerner founded the International Game Fishing Association (IGFA), which made the rules for heavy saltwater angling and still verifies and maintains its records. Some of them are remembered as the hook-and-line equivalents of Babe Ruth or Jack Nicklaus: S. Kip Farrington, Zane Grey, Alfred Glassell (the first man to take a billfish that weighed more than a thousand pounds on rod and reel), and of course Ernest Hemingway.

The tackle they used was enormous: The London firm of Hardy, then the reigning rod maker, made a steel-core pole known as a "Zane Grey" that weighed nearly three pounds and was the first to sport roller guides, locking ferrules, and other amenities of today's rods; the ponderous Vom Hofe reels, wound with half a mile of Ashaway line braided from Irish linen that terminated in a steel leader made by the same Roebling works that spun the cables for the Brooklyn Bridge, were like marine winches compared to modern gear. In fact, the rapid development of tackle worried Hemingway, who wrote in the introduction to Farrington's 1939 book on big-game fishing that the sport was in danger of being ruined by it, because it reduced the struggle involved in "a contest of strength and endurance between a man or a woman and an oversized fish."

The sporting essence of that struggle, as Hemingway set it forth, was the one whose elements are enshrined in the IGFA rules. The angler must bear the whole weight and pull of the fish by himself, holding the rod and reel in his own hands, with extra support from a harness across his back to which the gear could be attached. But he must not tie, rest, or prop the rod against any part of the boat, because then "he is not fishing—the boat is fishing for him"; instead of fighting the angler, the tuna or marlin is towing the boat. Nobody else on board may touch the rod or reel until the fish is at the boat and it's time to grab the leader. Some kinds of tackle were expressly forbidden, such as the low-gear, two-handled reels, like the "coffee grinders" used for tightening sail sheets on racing yachts, that enabled the fisherman to literally crank in a big fish instead of "pumping" it—raising the rod and then winning a yard or two of line by winding while lowering it, a tiring technique that pits the angler's muscular strength against the weight and resistance of the prey.

No one who has not tried it should underestimate either the subtlety or the hardship of big-game fishing. To be tied into a big marlin that will rip hundreds of yards of line from the reel in an unstoppable plunge to the depths of the ocean, and then have to pump him up, yard by hard-won yard to the surface, only to have him sound again and force you to repeat the struggle while the boat is rolling in a strong cross sea and your legs shake from hours of bracing them against the footrest of the fighting chair and your back muscles hurt and your left hand is numb from holding the rod grip and your right is an aching claw from turning the reel handle—this is one of the toughest forms of sport ever devised, and not to be scoffed at by those who have not done it.

It was far more extreme in the 1930s, when doughty American big-gamers such as Farrington and Michael Lerner would go after Atlantic swordfish and giant bluefin tuna (in those days, any bluefin under five hundred pounds was jocosely classed as a "midget") among the rocks and reefs of Nova Scotia, not in forty-foot big-game boats but in small dories, each rowed by one man, equipped with homemade swivel fighting chairs. With little or no inertia from the dories, which were light shells, it was the purest form of man-versus-fish angling, almost equally punishing to both.

This kind of fishing is no longer done, partly because it was so rough on the fisherman, but mainly because the fish are no longer there, whereas sixty years ago they schooled in incredible abundance. Farrington, in *Atlantic Game Fishing* (1939), casually mentions how Maine harpooners would go after giant bluefin tuna off Portland in the 1930s: The hunter "hopes that if he misses the mark the dart will strike the fish beneath the one at which he aimed. These great fish are usually found in layers three or four feet deep, travelling like a flotilla of submarines. Over five hundred fish a year are brought into the Portland piers. . . ." Nothing like this can be experienced in American waters today, or ever will be again.

Most fish become familiar if you go after them regularly. Yet not completely so, for each fish is new, and there are moments when the sense of strangeness revives and sits bolt upright; these are among the high points of any fisher's career. The one I remember most vividly happened off Montauk, at the eastern tip of Long Island, in the summer of 1985. I was on an overnight trip to fish for tuna on the Canyon, a part of the continental shelf about seventy miles out in the Atlantic, in a no-frills offshore boat skippered by an artist friend, Alan Shields. After the long night's run out, the sun rose golden and glorious out of the Atlantic and the sea was flat calm; you could see the smallest ripple a mile away. We set the trolling lines and the "bird," a teaser with two wings that fluttered on the surface sixty feet back from the stern and was supposed to excite the curiosity of fish. That done, there was nothing to do but wait. An hour later, nothing had come up. And then Alan saw something dead ahead: the unmistakable sickle fins of two giant bluefin tuna, hovering on the light-stricken surface as though sunning themselves. They were perhaps half a mile ahead. If we went past them at trolling speed, we would scare them down. There was probably no way of getting them to strike at a lure. But Alan wanted one of those fish (at the prices the Japanese were paying dockside at Montauk for prime bluefin, he could have paid for a whole season's fuel with it), and he decided to go after them with a harpoon. He would steer the boat and I would be up in the bow with the spear, whose detachable bronze head was already rigged to several hundred feet of line and an orange balloon buoy. There I would stand, intrepidly balanced out on the bow pulpit, as we treacherously sneaked up on the fish, and when I was within range, I would fling the harpoon into the tuna's vitals. There was only one snag about this arrangement. I am not Queequeg. My only experience of spearing fish was sniggling eels with a small trident. Of hitting a tuna from above with a ten-foot spear, I had no conception, and the fact that fishermen used to do this as a matter of course in their pursuit of tuna, swordfish, and other monsters of the deep off Montauk meant very little to me. I was a rank novice, a mere art critic, and (worse) an art critic who had read several cautionary yarns of what happens to incautious harpooners who happen by accident to get a coil of line around their arm, leg, or even neck as it comes burning out of the tub, pulled by a quarter-ton of potential sashimi, maddened with shock and pain, accelerating down and away into the oceanic abyss. Tuna can do sixty miles an hour. This thought hung before me as I drew closer to the fish, nervously balancing the shaft in my hand. I focused on the nearer fish. It seemed to hover in the water: the silver flanks, the dark blue back, not the leaden darkness of a dead fish, but alive, inexpressibly vital, the small dorsal finlets glowing yellow. Closer and closer. And then I caught its eye, that huge eye with its hypnotic black center, evolved to capture every last photon in the deep sea. God, it occurred to me, was looking at me through that fish. I was frozen. Dimly I heard a voice from the flying bridge behind me: "Stick him! Stick him!" But I couldn't; I couldn't imagine throwing the harpoon.

The eye had paralyzed me. Later I would learn from other fishermen, such as Peter Matthiessen, that this was not an uncommon occurrence. *Never look at the tuna's eye,* ran the conventional wisdom. Or at a swordfish's, either, which is even larger and more hypnotic. But I will never forget the sight of that bluefin, in the splendor of its unreflective life, or how it slid out of sight with the merest quiver of its body, cleanly accelerating through the blue, gone forever. It took Alan some time to forgive me.

By then I had been fishing around Long Island for several years. My interest in angling had gone flat and dormant when I left Australia for Europe in the early 1960s. In Italy, where I lived for a while in the fishing village of Porto Ercole, there were few fish to catch; even thirty-odd years ago, the waters of the Tyrrhenian Sea were so depleted by pollution and relentless dragnetting that a two-pound *dentice* or *spigola* would become the talk of the Bar Centrale. In England, where I settled later, I seldom moved outside London. No fishing there. But after I crossed to New York in 1970, fishing presented itself once again.

The eastern end of Long Island, three hours or less from Manhattan, was one of the world's great fisheries and, though considerably depleted, it still is. The angler's year there begins in April, when the "cocktail blues"—small bluefish—begin to show up in the bays and the flounder stir from their hibernation on the seabed, and it goes right through to the middle of November, when it gets too cold for me or any but the hardiest to fish from the beaches or from an open boat. Spotted silver weakfish (so called not for any debility, but because of the ease with which the hook tears from their mouth membranes) turn up in the early spring, and then there are runs of mackerel. In April the Greenport dock is crowded with Greek-Americans who come there to catch squid at night, with electric floodlights and jigs. In May and June the striped bass begin to appear. Bluefish last all summer and into the fall, and by July the fluke (a flatfish, like a flounder only fiercer and more carnivorous, running up to twelve or thirteen pounds, at which size they justify their nickname of "door mats") are to be caught all over the Peconic Bay system. With the warming of the offshore water come the tuna, though in badly diminished numbers these days: yellowfin, albacore, the "false albacore" or little tunny (known as "watermelons" for their thick, compact bodies and striped flanks), and the lord of them all, *Thunnus thynnus,* the Atlantic bluefin. The inshore fishing reaches a crescendo in September and October, with the schools of striped bass and still more bluefish, and the appearance of albacore and bonito in the bays.

The handsomest of all these fish, and the one most ardently pursued by anglers, is *Morone saxatilis*, the striped bass, with its silver-flanked body tinged with topaz bronze and striated by horizontal black lines, its fine proportions spoiled only, in the larger specimens, by a glutton's potbelly. It is also by far the best-tasting and the most amenable to any kind of cooking: poached, baked, grilled, fried, or sliced into sashimi when right out of the water. "An excellent fish," wrote Captain John Smith in 1614. "They are so large, the head of one will give a good eater a dinner, and for daintiness of diet they excell the Marybones [marrow bones] of Beefe. . . . I myselfe at the turning of the tyde have seen such multitudes passe . . . that it seemed to me that one mighte go over their backs drishod." The best eating size—the "money fish," as professional seiners used to call them—is six to ten pounds, but they grow much bigger, to sixty or seventy; the heaviest recorded specimen was a 125-pounder taken in 1891 in North Carolina. They were so common, and their migratory runs from their spawning grounds in the Chesapeake Bay system north along the Atlantic coast so huge, that for a time the English settlers of New England, taking their cue from the Indians, buried them in their fields as fertilizer. But as early as 1639 this practice was banned by the General Court of the Massachusetts Bay Colony—the first species-protection law ever passed in America. Striped bass also played a role in early American education, as in 1670 the Plymouth Colony used revenues from bass and mackerel to set up the New World's first public school.

One of the striper's great merits, from the angler's point of view, is its accessibility. In the southern Atlantic states they are known as "rockfish," because they prefer coastal waters and, with their muscular bodies and broad propeller tails, are superbly adapted to cope with the violent stresses of life among the reefs, rips, and beach surf. Stripers are anadromous, "up-going," which means that they ascend rivers to spawn—a hundred miles above the tidewater, in the case of the Roanoke River's spawning grounds—and can live quite happily in fresh water. Each year they do a mass migration along the land's edge, from the Chesapeake up to New Jersey, New York, Massachusetts, and Maine, and then return to their wintering grounds in the south. Sticking to the coast, they are easy to get at. At every point along their immemorial route, on every rock and headland and beach and in thousands of inshore boats, fishers are waiting for them, jigging, spinning, bait casting, trolling, sinker bouncing, and casting long streamer flies. This is quite a gauntlet to run, but since the bass do not venture far offshore they are not exposed to heavily industrial forms of fishing, the long lines and deep-sea nets that are decimating other species such as the tuna. The greater danger to coastwise fish is chemical pollution from runoff and sea dumping—not only on the open shore but, especially, in their southern spawning grounds and nursery waters. *Morone saxatilis'* Atlantic range runs along the most heavily industrialized and intensively farmed coast in America, and the witch's cocktail of pesticides, fertilizers, heavy metals, and ghastly polysyllabic chemical effluents that is sluiced and dumped from it almost beggars rational imagination. DDT, dieldrin, dibromochloropropane, PCBs, cadmium, arsenic, lead, hexachlorobenzene, cis-chlordane, mercury: All these and many more went into the salt water and from there into the livers, testes, and ova of the bass. It is not surprising that when John Coles wrote his admirable book *Striper* (1978) about the relations between *Morone saxatilis* and *Homo sapiens*, he felt driven to the most pessimistic of conclusions: "Ten years from now, at its current rate of decline, the striped bass . . . will have vanished as a viable species." But fortunately, this didn't happen.

In the last decade, strict limits have been placed on the taking of striped bass on Long Island. The minimum keeper size was fixed at thirty-three inches: an eighteen-pound fish, six years old (well into middle age, though tagged specimens have lived into their mid-twenties), and tasting—so anglers grumbled—like a copy of the Sunday edition of the *New York Times*, rolled up and boiled. The size restrictions caused prolonged and bitter controversy. They were denounced as a mere cosmetic by those (including Peter Matthiessen, nature writer, novelist, and a fisherman of long experience) who believed that the decline of the striper was due not to overfishing but to the chemical poisoning of the spawning grounds. Matthiessen wrote a powerful and evocative book, *Men's Lives* (1986), to defend the dwindling community of Long Island dory-seiners against charges brought by the sport-fishing lobby that it was they, not the amateur hook-and-liners, that put too much pressure on the bass population, and that in any case pollution was the real threat to the fish. Nobody could deny that pollution does their spawning and growth immense harm, but the fact is that the hardy and resilient bass have made a comeback in the last decade. Either their population crash was increased by a cyclical recession of unknown origin (this has been known to happen to bluefish as well as stripers) or else the massive catch of smaller specimens, mainly by hook-and-liners, really did tip the scales toward disaster. Whatever the case, since the size limits were imposed the bass population of eastern Long Island has recovered, and they are everywhere. This is one of the few really promising feats of wild-fish management that America has to show. Alas, the species that got driven out of business was the tiny band of dory-seiners who, like their ancestors for two centuries, had netted the Long Island beaches but, unlike the droves of sport fishermen, were in no way responsible for the crash.

The staple of Long Island sport fishing is *Pomatomus saltatrix*, the bluefish, the only representative of its family, the Pomatomidae. It assumes various names, depending on its age. Little ones are "snapper blues," young ones—up to two pounds or so—are "cocktail blues" or "tailors," and then you have regular "blues." The really big ones, which go to fourteen or fifteen pounds, are "gorillas." It is exactly the same fish that is known as a *pesce turco* in Italy and a *lufer* in Turkey, as a "tailor" in Australia and an *anchova* in Brazil. It is the fish that everyone knows how to catch because, given its habits and temperament, you don't need to know anything to catch one. Charter captains with their freight of inexperienced weekend tourists go out in flotillas off Montauk and around Shagwong Reef, into the Race between Fishers Island and Great Gull lighthouse, and in Plum Gut between Orient Point and Plum Island; they run out their wire lines, each with a four-armed umbrella rig trailing hooks adorned with red and green surgical tubing, and in come the blues. Wire-line trolling isn't fishing, it's winching. It doesn't deserve to be called a sport. Jigging for blues is somewhat higher on the evolutionary scale. To do this, you snap a jig—a shiny, spindle-shaped metal lure weighing up to half a pound—onto your wire leader, which is in turn tied to a thirty-pound monofilament line. You then click the reel into free spool, drop the jig over the side, and let it run down to the bottom, keeping your thumb on the spool to control backlash—a condition in which the spool turns faster than the line is going out, creating a horrible bird's nest. You feel the bump as the jig hits the bottom. You see the line go slack for an instant. You throw the reel into gear and crank as fast as you can. What you are hoping for is not a delicate touch, but a violent thump, as though a living cinder block had attached itself to your line. This is a bluefish, and you must now reel him in through a hundred or so vertical feet of water, while the tidal rip carries your boat along. Once the blue is on the surface, you swing him inboard and drop him on the deck, where he must be approached with care and resolution. Reputedly, unlike most fish, they can see out of water, and what they see and will bite is the hand that caught them. You must grab the beast behind the gills, hold him hard, twist the hook out of his jaw (no delicate dentistry here), and skid him into the fish well, then sluice down the blood, because it will dry as hard as crimson acrylic. Then run up against the tide, start your drift, and jig again. It is not the most refined form of fishing, but there is something agreeably basic and brutish about it, and women, I have noticed, love it; it speaks to the latent maenad in them.

The problem is not how to catch Long Island blues but what to do with them afterward. Catching one bluefish is like eating one french fry. If they are around, you always end up with more than you need, and bluefish are about as easy to give away in the summer as oversize zucchini: It's a form of generosity that your friends despise. They are an oily fish and don't freeze well—a late-season gorilla blue, fattened and glutted by gorging on menhaden and herring, is one of the greasiest brutes that swims. The epicure would say that bluefish are not even much good the day after they're caught, because their flesh is attacked by its own enzymes and quickly turns mushy. It is wholly pointless to buy them in a New York fish market, because they have already been out of the water for days. But caught in the morning, bled, gutted, filleted, and laid on the barbecue for lunch, with a handful of chives and some lemon juice, they can be memorable. The pleasures of eating them, though, pale beside those of catching them. Blues are voracious beyond belief. They're like Cuisinarts with fins, equipped with rows of razor teeth. A school of blues tearing into a school of baitfish on the surface is one of those spectacles that will still all thoughts of the benevolence and peaceability of Nature. It is manic, out-of-control *Mörderlust*—every fish a Jack the Ripper. You can see a feeding school miles away, from the birds—seagulls and terns wheeling and hitting the water, scarfing up the mangled bits of smaller fish that the blues are attacking. Old-timers say that if they're eating menhaden, you can smell them, too—the oil in the baitfish, released by the blues' jaws, makes a slick on the water. I can't claim to have noticed this, but right under the boat I have seen bluefish, glutted with their prey, vomit it all up like Roman gluttons before gorging again. When in such frenzies, blues will strike at practically anything from a streamer fly to a Budweiser can, and if they miss it, they will strike again. Once hooked, they fight with a furious all-out abandon that makes the classier and more fastidious striped bass look relatively sluggish. "If the species grew to the size of a bluefin tuna," declares the sober entry in *McClane's Fishing Encyclopedia*, "nothing could stand before it in the oceans of the world." No, indeed, it would be a sort of *T. rex* with fins, indomitably savage. Luckily for swimmers, the bluefish does not get that big—the largest recorded one, a forty-five-pound monster, was caught in a net off the coast of Africa, and the hook-and-line record, just under thirty-two pounds, was taken in Hatteras Inlet, North Carolina, in 1972.

No prestige, therefore, attaches to catching a bluefish. Often you have no say in the matter. It has happened, to my annoyance, when casting a fly for false albacore. These small members of the tuna family, the scombroids, turn up in the Long Island bay system in late summer and fall. Getting near them is very much a matter of luck. They travel in small schools and surface quite suddenly; then they dive again and vanish, and there is no way of knowing when they'll reemerge. So you have to be quick and accurate, and lay the fly in front of them as soon as you see them. Doing this while wobbling on the casting platform of a twenty-foot Keys flatboat in a moderate chop, with the wind over your wrong shoulder, is a test. At my level of skill, I can do it perhaps once in six tries—and you don't get six shots at albacore in an ordinary morning. Then, due to the unspeakable perversity of fate, the fish that grabs the fly turns out to be a solitary bluefish that gate-crashed the school of albies; by the time it is in the boat, juddering and glaring at you with its yellow assassin's eyes, the albacore are somewhere over the horizon. I have never yet caught a little tunny, or so much as hooked an albacore, on a fly rod. But next year will be different.

The excitement of connecting with a fish is in proportion to the hours of tedium that surround it, and the extreme case of this is another form of saltwater angling: fishing for tarpon. You can get blasé about blues, even about stripers, but tarpon—never. The tarpon, *Megalops atlanticus,* is a giant archaic herring, which grows to two hundred pounds or so. It is quite widely distributed on both sides of the Atlantic, from the Florida Keys down the Mexican coast, and on the other side along the flank of Africa. There, it attains great size but is rarely pursued by foreign anglers, who are understandably nervous of being shot in error by some AK-47–wielding teenager in the latest civil war in Sierra Leone. African anglers, their economy being what it is, can rarely afford tarpon gear, so the fish is safe there. It is hardly less secure on the coast of the Americas, but for other reasons. The food value of a tarpon is nil; its skeleton is a web of sharp, interwoven bones, and the flesh between them, when cooked, tastes uninteresting. Its sport value as a fly fisher's target, though, is unbeatable. This statement is a code. "Sport value" means that they are not only inedible but insanely expensive to pursue, and, if hooked, practically impossible to get to the boat—unless they jump into it of their own accord, breaking an angler's leg in the process, as they have been known to do. (A few anglers have actually been killed by falling tarpon.) Of course, tarpon can be taken by trolling, or with live bait—but then, I have seen Caribbean kids catching bonefish from a jetty in Grand Turk with hand lines and rusty hooks baited with conch. Such rudimentary means are spurned by fly rodders, who want to make life as hard as it can possibly be made.

The first stop on the *via crucis* of humiliation, then, is one of those specialized stores that sell fly-fishing gear of such cost and technological refinement that it feels a bit like shopping for a Formula One car. Every tarpon wanna-be has a favorite store; mine is the Urban Angler, in New York City. Procure a nine-foot, twelve-weight, three-piece carbon-Kevlar-graphite-Kryptonite Sage or Loomis rod ($600 or so) and a suitable reel. "Suitable" means that it must have room for a great deal of backing and cost not less (and preferably much more) than $600. A tarpon reel needs a drag system that won't fuse into a blob when the fish runs, and hence must be made of semiprecious metals and recondite alloys used only in the brakes of Ferraris or, perhaps, the entrails of the space shuttle. Then backing, and fly line, and leaders, and flies, and a pint of sunscreen, and a pair of those Polaroid glasses that cost, inch for inch, the same as a medieval stained-glass window in Sotheby's . . . Well, it could have been worse. You might have wanted to set yourself up for tuna. You are getting off relatively cheap, though this, as President Clinton might have said upon his sworn oath, depends on what you mean by *relatively*.

Now you are in, let's say, Islamorada, Florida. You have booked a guide and boat for three days. The first day was overcast and rainy, with a sharp chop on the water, and there was no point in even trying to go out, since the only way to catch a tarpon on fly is to see it coming from afar and cast to it; no fish can be seen in this leaden murk. You therefore spent the day reading an improving book, snoozing in the motel room, and eating conch fritters in a bar, a routine punctuated by re-assuring phone calls from your guide, who knows that tomorrow will be great. The second day is, if anything, worse and windier. But that night the front passes through, and the dawn of the third day looks like a picture postcard, gold, blue, and calm. Filled with the unreasoning optimism that is both the angler's folly and his main defense against go-ing wholly cuckoo, you meet Bud or Jake or Billy Bob down at the marina. His craft is a low-slung, open Keys casting boat, like a slipper twenty feet long, with a poling platform raised over its big outboard. Useless in the open sea, it is beautifully adapted to the shallow maze of cuts and channels where tarpon cruise. It skims for miles over the flats, hardly raising a wake. Your fate is deter-mined; it is all in the hands of the guide. Eventu-ally he stops where, being an expert, he knows tarpon will be: at the edge of a channel where they will come through, singly or in pods of five or ten, looking for food. He drives a long fiber-glass pole into the shallow bottom and ties the boat to it. Now you need only wait, as your excitement burns down into stoic resignation, while nothing happens and the skull-frying sun climbs higher into the sky. It is futile to repine.

Sometimes, however, they do appear. The guide can see them but you cannot, because you hardly know what you are looking for until it's too late. "Five or six at one o'clock, a hundred feet out," he drawls, with the merest whisper of an exclamation mark. You must now try to spot them through the dazzle of light on the water, and eventually you do: slender, dark logs, much smaller than they ought to look, coming straight at you across the confusing moiré pattern of the flat bottom. Meanwhile you are frantically stripping line from the reel, getting ready to throw the fly. What you should do next, calmly, deftly, and without delay, is put a sixty-foot shot a couple of yards in front of the lead fish and then start stripping line in so that it sees the fly moving through the water, mistakes it for a small fish, and hits. Fat chance. Flooded with adrenaline and buck fever, you do everything wrong. The line has got under your sneaker because, stupidly, you moved your foot, and it falls short. Or the fly drops behind the fish. Or the hook, thanks to your bad back-cast, snags your shirt or your earlobe. *"Il mondo e pieno,"* wrote Leonardo, *"d'infinite ragioni che non furono mai in isperienza"*: The world is full of infinite causes that were never experienced before. All too true; the tarpon have gone.

But once in a while a fish strikes. Amid a whoosh of surface foam, a giant mouth like a silver bucket opens and sucks the fly in. You strike back immediately, and whip the fly right out of the tarpon's mouth. Or you wait a second, strike, and connect. Just as you might put the cast right one time in three, and the fish might take the fly one time in five, so you might, with luck, get one hookup in three strikes. The odds thus far are not great: one in forty, and this is before the tarpon has even begun to fight.

They have jaws like cinder blocks, solid bone and gristle. Probably the hook will not hold. But if it does, both you and the tarpon are in trouble—you more than it. You realize this when the fish begins its run, and the slack line that had been lying on the carpeted foredeck hits the first rod guide in a knot. You claw it loose. It sizzles out, and suddenly the fish is on the reel. You are now attached to a creature of extraordinary strength and wildness, which tears all the fly line off the reel in a matter of seconds, and will be a hundred yards into the backing before you can recover your breath. It is common for a biggish tarpon—sixty pounds or more—to run for a couple of miles in long dashes before it is brought to boat (*if* it is), so the guide has no choice but to cast off from the pole and follow it around the flats. Its predicament, basically, is that it can run but not hide. The sand flats are shallow, rarely more than eight feet, so the tarpon cannot sound, and they contain no structure, such as rocks or wrecks or reefs, in which it can hole up and break the line. Since it cannot go down, it goes up, repeatedly. The jump of a tarpon is startling and scary. It can go as high as ten feet. The fish explodes out of the water, twisting and whipping, a column of quicksilver in a storm of foam. It is an epiphany. Nothing is more silver than a tarpon in the sunlit air. It hangs at the top of its arc and then crashes back into the sea. Then it does it again, and again. Short of a big billfish tail-walking, these acrobatics are the most exhilarating sight that fishing affords. If the leader doesn't snap or the hook pull out of the fish's mouth after these jumps, you probably have a good chance of getting the tarpon in. But it is a slugging fight all the way, and after the first half hour your rod arm begins to burn as though you've been chopping mahogany with a hatchet. If you do wear the tarpon down to the point where it comes alongside, and then release it, the relief is mutual. It would be absurd to kill it; better to be left with nothing but a photograph of its gleaming, ancient head and your beetroot-colored face. Do not, above all, think of having its corpse mounted as a trophy. Fish taxidermy is a steady business in Florida, but when you deliver your tarpon it won't come back stuffed. The real fish will be weighed, measured, and then ignominiously tossed in a Dumpster. You will receive, for many, many dollars more, a generic fiberglass tarpon, which are made as blanks in incremental sizes (100 pounds, 120 pounds, 140 pounds, and so on), air-brushed to silvery lifelikeness, and kept in storage by the taxidermist until some deluded angler brings in a fish of the right size. It would have been better to short-circuit the whole business and buy one direct from Friendly Freddy the Fish Stuffer. Some cheats do this. I used to know an art collector with a giant battleship of a house perched on the dunes at Easthampton. Over his fireplace hung a body mold of a billfish, purchased at a yard sale. Cannily, he neither claimed nor denied catching it. His nonfishing guests assumed the former; his fishing guests, who knew he wasn't a fisherman, thought it was by Damien Hirst or Jeff Koons. It was perfect: a postmodernist, virtual trophy of a combat that never happened, an ironic gloss on the importance of being Ernest Hemingway.

II

FRESH WATER

UNLIKELY AS IT MAY SEEM, my first identifi-
ably sexual memories are associated with fish
and fishing. Back in 1950, when I was eleven years
old, I came across a book in my father's library:
Salar the Salmon, by Henry Williamson. This short
and elaborately written book is sometimes referred
to as an "angling classic"—but actually it isn't
about angling at all, at least not from the viewpoint
of the angler. It is about life underwater, into
which human enemies sometimes intrude; it is a
novel whose central character is an Atlantic
salmon, ascending its home stream to spawn after
its long migration. It is pre-Disney, in that it contains no trace of the pathologically sentimental

grafting of human characteristics into nonhuman creatures that has overrun the childish imagination since Bambi, the fawn with no anus, first hit the silver screen. In its depiction of the Darwinian world in which sea creatures actually live, where everything is prey to everything else, it seemed alien and utterly fascinating. At the end of his odyssey, having run the gauntlet of seals, otters, nets, and a villainous lamprey, Salar finally reaches his biological Ithaca: the spawning beds, or "redds." There, a hen salmon named Gralaks— "ripe, ready to drop her eggs"—is scooping a trough in the gravel to spawn in. Salar moves in on her. "She jerked and shook on her side, as though trying to touch the back of her neck with her tail. Eggs dribbled quickly from her. . . . [Salar] moved forward, feeling as though he were being drawn from underneath by a lamprey of sweeter and sweeter sensation. His milt flowed from him in a mist. . . . For a few moments Salar lay in ecstasy on the redd." And, lucky devil, he just keeps going.

As the days went on Salar became heavy with weariness. Most of his milt was shed; in slow pulse after slow pulse his life's sweetness had been drawn from him, leaving with each emptiness a greater inflaming desire, which during the day lapped about the wasted body with dreams of an everlasting sea of rest; but when darkness came, and the water was ashine with stars, he felt himself running bright with the river, and sweetness returned to him on the redd beside Gralaks.

Phew. A tad overwrought, you may think, though I didn't at the time. A flagrant bit of RBP (rich, beautiful prose) it may be, though not inherently sillier than the sex scenes in *Lady Chatterley's Lover*, which of course I had never even heard of. Perhaps you had to be there—a preteen with unidentified longings beginning to stir in him, in a family and a culture that were single-mindedly bent on maintaining his purity for as long as possible. In Australia in 1950 there were no sex manuals, magazines full of naked girls with staples in their navels, or novels with "explicit" passages. Even less could you download, from the Web, pictures of alleged schoolgirls doing weird things with enormously endowed ponies. Such improvements were far in the future. The strictest censorship reigned in civil life, and in Catholic life it was even stricter. One was meant to confess one's "impure thoughts" to the priest, but this I never did. Somehow it just seemed too complicated to explain to Monsignor O'Regan, in the dark and stuffy confines of the confessional booth of Saint Mary Magdalen's at Rose Bay, how I had been led to them by a description of spawning fish. He might have thought I was some kind of pervert in the making, not just an ordinary prepubescent sinner. It was one thing to risk the fires of hell, but quite another to look like a fool. Besides which, although Henry Williamson had told me what fish got up to, I was still far from clear about what people did.

The other memory comes from 1952, the year after my father died, when I was thirteen. Gradually the clutter of stuff he left behind him in cupboards and drawers had been winnowed out: rods and guns going to my elder brothers, clothes sent to Catholic charities. But a lot of small things remained, and since nobody wanted to throw them away, I would sometimes paw circumspectly through the contents of the drawers, trying to recover some detail or other of the life of a man whom I deeply loved but now would never know as an adult. It was in this way that I came across the first visual image of a seminaked woman that I had ever seen. It was not a photograph. It was molded, in clear Lucite, on the spool on which an American fly-fishing line had been coiled. The brand name was Rain-Beau, a pun in Art Deco lettering. I forget the manufacturer's name. It had been made in some place called Milwaukee, far away in unimaginable America. Lucky Americans, to have such things on their fishing gear! The scene was a river, with Lucite eddies flowing past Lucite rocks. Smack in the center, next to a rock, was the girl. Her actual height was perhaps two inches, but she looked willowy and, I was sure, tall. A mane of hair cascaded down her back, coiling like the eddies in the water. Though it was Lucite, I was convinced she was blond. She was fly-fishing. Her rod was bent in an arc under the pull of a trout, which could be seen leaping. Her backside and legs were hidden, although suggestively, in waders. But you could see her bare back and, most important, the profile of her breast. It was perky and, as such dimensions go in two-inch-high girls, quite large. I thought her mysterious and entrancing—a sexpot nymph of the stream. (Indeed, from then on I could not hear the word *nymph* uttered, as it often is by fly fishers, without thinking of her.) For sure, you never saw girls like that on Rose Bay pier, only other scrubby small boys with freckles, rugby scabs, and hand lines, along with a few old codgers on the dole. Unconsciously, I suppose, I thought of her as a reward of the more refined and difficult kind of fishing that had begun to invade my imagination: fishing with a fly in rivers, not with bait in the sea.

For by then I was deep into fly fishing, more in theory than in everyday practice, since there were no trout-bearing rivers near Sydney. My father had been a keen fly fisherman, and so were my elder brothers. He was a strict purist when it came to any sport, but particularly about shooting and fishing. *Assume that any gun you touch is loaded. Never point it at anything you don't intend to shoot at. Never shoot anything alive unless you mean to eat it. And never, under any circumstances, fish for trout with anything but a fly.* This prohibition had both practical and moral aspects. The practical one was that fly fishing was usually a more effective way to catch trout than live-baiting: You could, indeed must, figure out what they were feeding on and then choose a fly to match the food, whether that happened to be larvae on the stream bottom, smaller fish, or insects descending on the water. Your fly box, with its wide palette of different patterns, gave you the means to do this more efficiently, and of course more elegantly, than barging around on the riverbank catching beetles in your hat. The moral aspect was related to the elegance.

From the time I was seven or eight, after my father had been released from service as a flying instructor in the Royal Air Force, the whole family—or as much of it as could be assembled—would go camping together on the Murrumbidgee River, in a valley named Yaouk, near Jindabyne, three hundred miles south of Sydney, in the foothills of the Australian Alps. The tent—a many-roomed structure of heavy canvas, with a bewildering array of poles, pegs, and guy ropes—would be packed into a two-wheeled trailer, along with the rest of the gear: grill, bush oven, kerosene lamps, Primus stove, cooking utensils, a folding table and chairs, rod cases, a pair of shotguns, a .22 single-shot rifle, duffel bags of clothes, food, books, and the Thunderbox, a folding single-hole wooden lavatory seat. The Hughes clan did not travel light, and this mass of stuff, tarped over and roped down, rose quite high above the sides of the trailer. It was as if we were heading for Africa, though without native bearers. The whole she-bang was then hitched to the family car, a turtle-like machine called a Chrysler Airflow. We would pack ourselves in and set off. Due to the primitive state of Australian roads then, the trip would take ten hours, evening to breakfast time, with occasional stops for car sickness. But it was worth it.

One arrived in the dry crackling paradise of the Australian bush: a golden valley, resonant with bird-calls, through which the Murrumbidgee flowed gin-clear over its pebbled bed, with backwaters full of undisturbed wild duck. It took all morning to unpack and raise the tent, and then there was lunch, but by afternoon we'd be free to fish.

Not that I was—at first. At nine I was not old and responsible enough to have a trout rod of my own. These rods were precious and, in post-war Australia, irreplaceable. They were exquisitely slender, three-piece split-cane rods, handmade before the war by the London firm of Hardy's. The days of the mass-produced fiberglass or, later, boron-graphite fly rod were far in the future. Cane rods were inordinately prone to damage, and a whole etiquette of handling attached to them. You couldn't lay one on the ground, in case you stepped on it and broke it. You had to lean it up against a tree, always vertical. Walking to the river, you had to carry the rod in three pieces, never assembled, so as not to run the tip into a bush and bust it. And so on and so forth; a samurai in dealing with his sword could hardly have been more circumscribed by ritual usage. The first year I went to Yaouk I was not allowed to touch the rods, though I would do so, surreptitiously, marveling at their lightness and finesse. The second year I was allowed to practice casting, always under adult supervision. Not until my third visit there was I turned loose on the water, on my own. The result was not good.

I can see the pool still, of course. Half a mile upstream from camp, with perfect solitude and a silence broken only by a crow saying at intervals, as Australian crows morosely do, *fark*. Thirty feet wide, glass-clear, with deep dark overhangs. In the middle, several rocks; and behind each of them, hanging in the eddy, a trout, just like the ones I had studied in the river before and scrutinized in the diagrams of my various trout books. Except that now I had a rod and some flies. All over the pool, fish were rising, not just dimpling the surface with demure rings, but slashing at the grasshoppers falling into the stream. The air was alive with grasshoppers. All thumbs, I managed to tie a fly to my leader. The first clumsy cast snagged me in a bush. The second, in a gum tree. The third landed in an ugly hurrah's nest of tangles on the water. The fourth, likewise. It was a nightmare. And when I finally got some semblance of rhythm into my casting, the trout ignored the flies, which didn't look like grasshoppers. This went on for half an hour, maybe more. Finally, sweating with frustration, I decided to break the great taboo. I got out my pocketknife, scraped the feathers off the largest fly I had, knotted the bare hook on, and impaled a fat, kicking hopper on it. Then I flipped it into the water. It floated, struggling, past the nearest rock. Instantly there was a swirl and, for the first time in my life, I was connected to a trout, and through it to the rest of the universe. It wasn't a giant—a brown, maybe two pounds—but it fought like a Kilkenny cat, making long, erratic runs and jumping into the air to show its golden spotted flanks. I did everything right. I dipped the rod tip when it jumped. I didn't freeze on the reel when it ran. I led sideways to tire the fish more. I knew what it was going to do and saw everything it did. I was in ecstasy. And at last, having fumbled the landing net from the hook on my belt, I was floating the exhausted fish into the mesh when the voice of Jehovah fell on me, like a ton of bricks, from the sky.

"Let that fish go!" it commanded.

I straightened up and looked wildly about me. Nothing. Then, to my horror, the head and chest of my father rose into view from where he had been watching everything I did, behind a big fallen eucalyptus trunk on the far bank.

"Release that fish!" he boomed.

I twisted the hook from its jaw and watched it half drift, half swim away downstream.

"Now come over here."

Filled with foreboding, I waded across the pool. I noticed, with worse foreboding, that Dad had unbuckled his belt and was pulling it out of the loops. He gently took the rod from my hand, leaned it carefully against the fallen trunk, and then less gently seized my arm, spun me around, and delivered a slashing stroke of the belt to my backside. It didn't hurt much.

"I saw that," he said grimly. "You got that trout with a hopper. You will never do that again. People who use live bait on trout are not fit to fish. They are thugs. They are barbarians. They might as well be using dynamite. Now, get back to camp."

Sniveling, hot with shame, I followed him. I was allowed back on the river the next day, and I have never since fished for trout with anything but an artificial fly. Perhaps in some spirit of expiation toward the god of fishing purity, I began to transfer the hobby mania that kids are apt to have away from building model airplanes and onto the tying of trout flies. There were copious examples at home, together with pattern books and the gear you needed to make flies: a tiny vise with pointed jaws to hold the hooks, forceps, thread, wax, varnish to seal the final knot behind the hook's eye, and dozens of small cellophane envelopes containing feathers. I turned them out by the score, perky confections of fluff and hackle that, for all I knew, had no similarity to Australian insects; but the ritual, that was what mattered. And sometimes they worked. The first time I caught a trout on a fly of my own making was on a stream called Spencer's Creek, a tributary of the Snowy River that flowed down a bony, bare hillside near Mount Kosciusko, the highest peak in Australia. I remember the near-abstract perfection of that stream: no entangling bushes, just big ledges of elephant-gray rock, snow-worn into gentle voluminous curves with sudden facets where the boulders had broken off, with the hillside mantled in wiry flattened grass and snow daisies rising out of the water. I was thirteen and fishing on my own, having walked a long way in from the road. There was a pool, maybe a hundred yards long, clear as green glass. I looked down on it from a smooth spur of granite. And there, hovering behind a large sunken rock, was a big trout. These elements—fish, rock, water, landscape—came together with astounding clarity, and I felt like their possessor. To complete the circle I must catch the fish with a fly I had tied myself, and no other would do. I picked out a March Brown, knotted it to the leader, and made one cast. I felt what tennis players or golfers do when the stroke is as sweet as it can be. The line shot out with a slight upstream curve; the leader turned over just as the books said it should; the fly parachuted softly onto the water, the transparent current bore it past the rock, and the fish rose to it. Fifteen minutes later I had him on the bank: a deep-bodied rainbow. I made a fire of snow-gum twigs and, when it had burned down, roasted him in the embers for lunch. The charred skin and scales came clean away, and his flesh was a deep pink from his diet of crayfish. I ate every scrap of him. I had never tasted anything as delicious, or as sacramental. Later, on the way back to the road, it occurred to me that I had at last done something, in relation to fish, of which my father would have fully approved. But he was dead, and beyond approving anything.

That fixed belief in the superiority of fly fishing for trout over all other ways of angling, held by my father and so many others like him—where did it come from? Evidently, class. It hardly existed before the English, in the nineteenth century, turned it into a mystique. Then it spread from England to America, and to the rest of the European-based world.

The earliest known reference to fly fishing occurs in *De Natura Animalium* (On the Nature of Animals) by Aelian, a Roman writer of the late second and early third centuries A.D., who described how it was done by Macedonians on a river called the Astraeus. The fish in question may or may not have been trout, but they were partial to a large insect locally known as a *hippurus*, resembling a bumblebee but useless as bait because its delicate wings shriveled at human touch. So the cunning Macedonians "wrap the hook in scarlet wool, and to the wool they attach two feathers that grow beneath a cock's wattles and are the color of wax"—producing a beelike, furry-bodied fly with wings. This, Aelian says, deceived the fish every time. He makes no claim that this was a "nobler" way of catching fish, only that it worked. There was no noble way of taking fish, because fish themselves weren't noble. Their pursuit was an entirely plebeian occupation.

Hunting was noble, the sport of kings and of gods. It was a means of transcendence. You proved your heroism, your fitness to command, by going up against, say, a wild boar in the woods of Thessaly with a spear. The ancient world assigned no imputation of bravery to catching mullet. Compared to the body of myth and legend that gathered around hunting, the ancient symbolism of fishing is quite meager.

This would change with the coming of Christianity. But it remains a mystery why the fish became a Christian symbol. Its precedents were slight. The Syrians, for instance, had a religious respect for fish that, according to Xenophon (*Anabasis* 1.4.9) impressed the Greeks; the ritual sacrifice of fish was not uncommon in the ancient world, and in particular it was part of Roman ceremonies of appeasement of the early fire god Vulcan. In the summer, the hottest part of the year, live fish taken from the Tiber would be thrown into a fire. This offering to Vulcan of wet creatures normally safe from his doings must have been meant to induce him to spare his natural prey, like summer crops or the dry structure of houses. But there was no fish god, or god who was part fish, in the Roman or Greek pantheons, though of course the sea had its own deities, starting with the Greek Poseidon (known to the Romans as Neptune).

To the Roman nobs, fishing was bucolic and uninteresting, and fishermen belonged with shepherds, laborers, and peasants, just above slaves. To the literate and influential, these people were so far down the social scale that they were not fully human and could be made into an amusing, "instructive" spectacle: illiterate, scarred by age and work, figures in an idyll. They could be scanned with an appreciative eye, but without the slightest fellow feeling, becoming the subject of genre sculpture for the patrician arcade or garden: the old fisherman carrying his creel, with withered flesh and ropy muscles, was a common type, and one such sculpture, in the collection of the Vatican Museums, was wrongly supposed for many years to represent the aged Seneca. This philosopher-dramatist, who preached moderation but accumulated a huge fortune in his hypocritical greed and toadying to the imperial court, would not have been pleased to be taken for a prole.

In the ancient world and the early Christian era, practically no one seems to have fished for pleasure. The ancient Romans were big fish-eaters, and the more extravagant among them laid out huge sums on private fish ponds. However, the only ancient Roman—certainly the only powerful one—known to have fished for sport was Mark Antony, who, according to Plutarch, went angling in the harbor of Alexandria with Cleopatra, and cheated at it: He paid some local fishermen in advance to dive under their barge and snag live fish on his hook, so as to cut a *bella figura* in front of his temptress. Cleopatra, once she caught on, paid him back by having her own slaves sneak down into the water and impale a salted fish on Antony's hook, much to the glee of the courtiers. And this pretense of fishing, to judge from Plutarch's account, was part of a pattern of social transvestism the two lovers enjoyed—they would also go slumming incognito late at night, getting into scrapes with the lower classes.

"Piso's a Christian, he worships a fish / There'd be no kissing if he had his wish," complains W. H. Auden's line soldier, scratching his lice on Hadrian's Wall. Probably the early Christian identification of Jesus Christ with a fish (in Greek, *ichthys*) came—like Christianity itself—from the Middle East rather than Rome. It was made more popular and memorable among early converts by becoming an acronym for their coded profession of faith: I [esos] Ch [ristos] Th [eou] U [ios] S [oter]— "Jesus Christ, son of God, Savior." Perhaps the image of the fish, elusive and slippery, also suited a clandestine religious cult persecuted by authority.

But Christ and his first followers, as readers of the Bible well know, weren't just fish but fishermen. Four of the apostles (Andrew, James, John, and of course Peter) were busy at the tedious work of net mending by the Sea of Galilee when Christ recruited them by offering to make them "fishers of men"; from then on, the image of the evangelist fishing for souls would proliferate throughout the religious imagery of the West. It had strong plebeian associations. Fishing was work—hard, sometimes dangerous, uncertain in its returns, meager in its profits. Almost all of it was done with nets. Hence the fishing net, for Christians, became identified with virtuous labor. Nets were honest; they did not deceive the fish. You dragged them through the water, but they didn't lure the prey into them. This was an important symbolic point when it came to depicting the various Christianized forms of fishing. Souls were swept up, gathered in the net of doctrine and faith. That they were all together in the net symbolized the community of the Church. That fish swam into the net of their own accord chimed with the Catholic doctrine of free will, of voluntary acceptance of the gospel truth. "In this Sea," preached John Donne, in a sermon he gave in Saint Paul's in 1619,

are we made fishers of men: of Men in generall: not of rich men, to profit by them, nor of poore men, to pierce them the more sharply, because affliction hath opened a way into them; Not of learned men, to be over-glad of their approbation of our labours, Nor of ignorant men, to affect them with an astonishment, or an admiration of our gifts; But we are fishers of men, of all men, of that which makes them men, their souls. And for this fishing in this Sea, this Gospel is our net.

Any means of catching the soul other than the direct and all-inclusive, netlike word of God must verge on the diabolic: "Eloquence is not our net: Traditions of men are not our nets; only the Gospel is." But angling, fishing with a rod and line and bait—that was a different matter. It entailed deception and guile in that the hook was hidden; the angler was archetypally a liar. "The Devil angles with hooks and bayts; he deceives, and he wounds in the catching; for every sin hath his sting."

For this reason, neither Christ nor any of his apostles was ever depicted "fishing for men" with a rod and line. The only exceptions to this were medieval images of God the Father angling for Leviathan, using Christ as bait and the cross as a hook. But that was fair, since Leviathan, the sea monster of the Nile, was by then fused with the image of Satan, himself the father of lies, and one could kill a liar by cunning, using Satan's own wiles to defeat him.

There was no such moral contrast between net and hook in the East, and in both China and Japan fishing was considered a worthy relaxation for scholars, courtiers, and aristocrats long before it became so in Europe. Japanese nobles of the Momoyama period built ornamented pavilions by their ponds, so that they could fish for carp. Chinese ink paintings depicted sages thinking, presumably, of philosophical matters while dangling a hair-thin line in the water. Verses extolled the freedom from mundane worries implied by fishing, and some, like Po Chu-I, even said it didn't matter whether one caught a fish or not:

> I, when I have come to cast my hook in the
>   stream,
> Have no thought of either fish or men.
> Lacking the skill to capture either prey
> I can only bask in the autumn water's light.
> When I tire of this, my fishing also stops;
> I go to my home and drink my cup of wine.

Perhaps because fishing in China was a high-class sport as well as common work, Chinese anglers were far ahead of European techniques. In Europe, angling with a rod and line had been practiced since about 300 B.C. But the line was fixed to the rod, whose length determined the scope of the angler's throw. Playing a fish by letting it take line and then recovering it was unknown. You had to depend on the springiness of the rod and the strength of the line. Izaak Walton claimed that the best strategy with a strong-running fish on a fixed line was to toss the rod into the water and let the fish drag it around until it tired. This is palpable nonsense, and not even his disciple Charles Cotton believed it. Long before, the inventive Chinese came up with a better idea: the fishing reel, wound with a running line. Probably it developed out of silk technology: Joseph Needham, the great scholar of Chinese science, speculated that someone had the bright idea of adapting a winding bobbin to use as a small winch. But whatever their origins, unmistakable fishing reels, attached to rods fitted with line guides, were turning up in Chinese paintings by the thirteenth century A.D. Not until the mid–seventeenth century do they appear in England. The first English writer to mention a reel was Thomas Barker, in *The Art of Angling* (1651); two years later Walton, a garrulous giver of technical advice, mentions that some salmon fishers "use a wheel about the middle of their rod, or near their hand, which is to be observed better by seeing one of them, than by a large demonstration of words."

The West, too, was slower to grasp the possibilities of fishing as something other than work—as a pastime, a mode of contemplation, or (as the subtitle to Walton's *The Compleat Angler* puts it) "the contemplative man's recreation."

The first piece of Western writing to enshrine this idea is in the *Book of St. Albans*, printed at Westminster in 1496 by the aptly named publisher Wynkyn de Worde. It is an essay titled "A Treatyse of Fysshynge with an Angle." Its author is unknown; traditionally it was ascribed to a noblewoman who had become a nun, Dame Juliana Berners, but there seems to be no evidence that she actually wrote it, if indeed she existed at all. No matter: "A Treatyse" is the starting point of all fishing literature in English. It would be copied, quoted, and plagiarized (most notably by Izaak Walton in *The Compleat Angler*, the most frequently reprinted book of all time next to the Bible and *Pilgrim's Progress*, but also by such ponderous luminaries as Robert Burton in *The Anatomy of Melancholy*) for the next three hundred years. Its basic message is that fishing is good for you, that it leads to health, long life, and virtue. Not so with commercial netting, whose long hours in bad weather can be the source of "grete Infirmytees." The netman can lose his tackle and his money with it, but all an angler stands to lose is a line and a hook—and perhaps a fish, if it breaks off. This, the author says, is "not grievous." ("Depends on the fish," another angler might mutter.)

What Dame Juliana clearly admires is the modest self-sufficiency of the angler, compared to the showier and more elitist rituals of the Plantagenet hunter or falconer. The angler walks and looks, takes in the landscape and its creatures without disturbing either. "A sweet air of the sweet savor of the meadow flowers"—I am modernizing the usage—"that makes him hungry. He hears the melodious harmony of birds. He sees the young swans, herons, ducks, coots and many other birds with their broods: which seems better to me than all the noise of hounds, the blast of horns . . . that hunters, falconers and fowlers can make." The angler must get up early, which, Dame Juliana optimistically thinks, "shall cause him to be holy." Fishing is good for the body, too, and for one's material estate, "for it shall make him rich." (There has never been any evidence that the last is true; the only people who have ever made a buck off amateur fishing are the makers of fishing gear, unless you include those impaired souls who lay bets on the outcome of a day's angling. As for holiness, I'd be the last to dispute the spiritual benefits of fishing, but it is also a great source of sin: taking the Lord's name in vain, filthy language, envy, and, above all, lying.)

These benefits imply duties. Dame Juliana was the first fishing writer in English to stress what we now call eco-responsibility and to sketch a code of behavior for anglers. Don't trespass on any "poore mannes" pond or stream, don't disturb his fish traps—or heinous and unsporting thought—steal the fish from them, even if they're in common water. Close the gates behind you and try not to step on the eggs of waterfowl. Don't go fishing with a whole bunch of people, as their company will distract you from meditation and prayer. Above all, don't take more fish than you need, because that will ruin the sport for yourself and others. Such admonitions, like the warnings given in fifteenth-century etiquette books—don't spit on the floor during dinner, don't blow your nose on the napkin or pick it at the table—may tell us something about the actual state of fishing customs in late Gothic England. They still hold true. Dame Juliana was the mother superior of bag limits and catch-and-release.

She also set a tone, which transmitted itself to later fishing writers—not that the genre got very big until the nineteenth century. Fishing didn't have the arrogance of "noble" hunting, and you didn't have to be rich to do it; all you needed was leisure, which connoted some independence of means, but certainly not the security of the landed gentry. (The poor did not hunt; they "poached," and were hanged or transported for it.) You might almost call it democratic, if democracy had existed in Izaak Walton's time. Its ultimate object was not to fill a bag with fish, but to acquire a closeness to Nature and a certain inner balance; "study to be quiet" was the motto of *The Compleat Angler* Au gling dissolved the long debate over whether the *vita activa* (the active life, that of the hero) or the *vita contemplativa* (the reflective one of the philosopher or anchorite) was better, because it was both. Angling was amateur, and it supplied a refined pleasure not to be had from netting, tickling, trapping, gaffing, stunning, or poisoning fish. The mild Walton gets severe on those unsporting souls who go after trout at night with torches and

spears: "This kind of way they catch very many:
but I would not believe it till I was an eyewitness
of it, nor do I like it now that I have seen it." His
disciple Charles Cotton, who added the section on
fly fishing to *The Compleat Angler*, is more forth-
right, inveighing against the ruin of rivers by "the
basest sort of people, by those unlawful ways of
fire and netting in the night, and of damming,
groping, spearing, hanging and hooking by day!
which are now grown so common, that, although
we have very good laws to punish such offenders,
every rascal does it." The angler does not sell his
fish; he eats them with friends, or gives them away
to passing milkmaids, who sing songs for him in
exchange for their supper. "Marry, God requite
you, Sir," effuses one of these pastoral nymphs in
The Compleat Angler, on accepting a chub,

> and we'll eat it cheerfully; and if you come
> this way a-fishing two months hence, a-
> grace of God I'll give you a syllabub of
> new verjuice in a new-made hay-cock for
> it, and my Maudlin shall sing you one of
> her best ballads; for she and I both love
> all Anglers, they be such honest, civil,
> quiet men.

She then warbles a song by Christopher Marlowe, "Come live with me, and be my love." It isn't exactly social realism, but never mind. What Walton is creating is a conventional idyll set in an English Eden. He is following, naturally enough for a man of his time and education, in the footsteps not only of Dame Juliana but of ancient Roman writers singing the blessings of the contemplative life in rural retreat, *"procul negotiis, ut prisca gens mortalium,"* in Horace's words—far from business worries, like the first race of mortals. He bridles at the idea, held by some desensitized souls, that fishermen are nitwits. No, no, sir, the boot is on the other foot, Piscator the fisher tells Auceps the falconer:

> And for you that have heard many grave, serious men pity Anglers, let me tell you, Sir, there be many men that are by others taken to be serious and grave men, which we contemn and pity. Men that are taken to be grave, because nature hath made them of a sour complexion, money-getting men,—men that spend all their time first in getting, then in anxious care to keep it; men that are condemned to be rich, and then always busy or discontented; for these

poor-rich-men, we Anglers pity them perfectly. . . . No, no, Sir, we enjoy a contentedness above the reach of such dispositions.

Not only did Walton like an idyll, but, as Howell Raines points out in his introduction to a recent edition of *The Compleat Angler*, he needed one. As a loyal monarchist, he had fled from London into rural seclusion in 1643–44, when Cromwell and the Puritans began to get the upper hand, and his "appreciation of the pastoral beauties of the streamside and the milkmaid's sweet songs was no doubt sharpened by the fact that . . . [he] was sticking hooks into worms rather than having his own head displayed on the end of a New Model Army pike."

But Walton's idyll did not have a hierarchy of prey. Walton would as soon have taken a decent-size tench as any salmon or trout. The segregation of "coarse" fish, from the tiny bleak, gudgeon, or stickleback on up to the obese carp, and their consignment to lower-class sport, had not yet begun. Nor had the corresponding elevation of trout and salmon. But one sees it beginning in Cotton's postscript to *The Compleat Angler*: "Doubtless, a Trout affords the most pleasure to the Angler of any sort of fish whatever; and the best Trouts must

needs make the best sport." Still, until the beginning of the nineteenth century salmon were
among the commonest of English fish, and cheap,
too: workers and laborers would complain if they
were given them to eat too often, and the same
applied to oysters, which in Samuel Pepys's day cost
pennies a barrel. (On the same principle, English
line soldiers in the Crimean War bitterly resented
being issued rations of a black, fishy, granular jam
in place of their regular bully beef. It was caviar.)

Just how the salmonids—trout, salmon, char,
grayling, and their various relatives—came to be
regarded as aristocratic game fish and the numerous
other freshwater species as coarse is an interesting
question with no simple answer, but no sociologist
(or none that I can find) seems to have gone deeply
into it. The discrimination began in the late eighteenth century and had become fixed in England
by the mid-nineteenth. My own guess—perhaps a
rather obvious one—is that it descended from the
intense concern with property laws in Georgian
England. Stable property, and the absolute right to
control public access to it, was one of the prime
clear signs of social stability for a landowning class
that often felt threatened from below by agrarian
unrest. One of the highest marks of a desirable
landholding was that, to use a much later phrase, "a

river runs through it," and that this river should
hold fish, whose safety from proletarian intrusion
must be upheld by law. Georgian England wit-
nessed a continuous struggle between fish thieves
and fish owners, spurred not so much by the economic importance of the fish to the landowner as
by its symbolic value. The monster of all property
acts, the Waltham Black Act of 1722, was passed
in response to some minor agrarian uprisings in
Hampshire, and it prescribed the gallows for some
two hundred different offenses to property, including the theft of live fish from streams and ponds—
this at a time when attempted murder of live
humans was still classed only as a misdemeanor. In
English social portraiture, the creel of freshly
caught trout joined the game bag of dead fur and
feathers as one of the marks of the gentleman, at
ease in his acres.

As the English countryside was transformed by
the Industrial Revolution, both the old landed
gentry and the new mercantile one whose coal
mines and iron works were fouling the streams and
blackening the meadows of an earlier England
naturally wanted to have their own unpolluted
crystal rills, the image of whose purity was the
trout. It was an Arcadian fish, which could only
live in clear running water, unlike the lowly tench

or carp, which could stand any amount of mud and gunk. Its flesh was firm and delicious. It looked supremely elegant, with its quicksilver flanks and rosy speckles. Its proportions were refined and its presence mild and elusive (the grayling was also called an umber, from *umbra*, Latin for "shadow"). Trout were fastidious. They spooked easily, thus summoning from the fisherman his reserves of those gentlemanly qualities, delicacy and circumspection. To fish "fine and far" (with a light leader, standing well back and making a long cast) was first enjoined by Cotton as a practical technique; by the nineteenth century it had become a stylistic imperative, a sign of class, like keeping a straight bat at cricket, which was also in those days a gentleman's sport. Trout fought bravely but surrendered gracefully. Once in hand, they could not jag you with spines, cut you with their gill covers, or inflict bites with their teeth. Nor were they covered with thick slime. The gear of fly fishing was clean, minimal. One handled a neat little tuft of feathers. One did not have to bother with the sometimes noisome baits used for coarse fish: slimy minnows, smelly pastes, the "ground-bait" or chum, or especially the pallid maggots, known euphemistically as "gentles," associated with corruption and the grave. (You wouldn't want to know what went into some of those compound baits. One seventeenth-century recipe included human fat and powdered bones, "mummy," cat fat, and grave earth—everything but Tartar's lips and the liver of a blaspheming Jew.)

The whole iconography of trout fishing befitted a gentleman—that is, a person of independent income, preferably landed, with ample leisure and a calm, philosophical disposition. Such a man, wrote James Saunders in *The Compleat Fisherman* (1724), "must have all his Passions at his Command, he must govern his Temper with an absolute Sway, and be able to sustain his Mind under the greatest Disappointments." In sum, he ought not stamp on his rods in frustration, curse and swear, or—as one particularly gross Australian media mogul did in the presence of a friend of mine in Alaska a few years ago—yank out a hogleg .44 Magnum and blow to shreds a landed salmon in pettish rage at being told he must release it. The true gentleman angler could not, by Saunders's reckoning, be a "Man of Business," because if he left his countinghouse to go fishing he "makes the Sport become a Vice in his Morals; his Angling is a Crime." Nor should he make fishing into a business, which lowered its tone. Such assumptions permeated the English literature of angling, which grew large through the nineteenth century and into the twentieth. Not only was the artificial fly better than natural bait, but the dry fly, which floated on the surface of the water, was morally superior to the wet fly, which did not; and both had a stylistic edge over the nymph, which had no wings and drifted along the bottom, emulating the larval stage of the insect. To catch a trout on a tiny fly, tied on a #16 or even #18 hook attached to a leader of gossamer thinness, was clearly a more elegant achievement than getting one on larger tackle. In due course, the whole Victorian-Edwardian Bushido of fine-tackle, dry-fly fishing would migrate from the chalk streams of Kent to the rivers of America, where it grew enormously. The chief transmitter of this fanaticism was an Englishman, Frederic M. Halford, whose bizarrely snobbish book *Dry-Fly Fishing in Theory and Practice* (1889) won numerous converts in the United States. Though they got rid of Lord North and George III long ago, Americans are ravenous for Anglo-derived signs of style, and large businesses, such as Ralph Lauren's fashion empire, have been raised on packaging these fictions to eager customers. Hence the annual appearance on the rivers of

New England, such as the Battenkill, of dedicated anglers wielding implausibly fragile two-weight rods, preferably made of old-fashioned bamboo rather than state-of-the-art synthetics. With these they "present" (the verb, with its ceremonious aura, is significant) diminutive flies to trout rarely more than a pound in weight—fish so jaded from being caught and released that they can tell an Orvis-tied Grey Wulff or Rat-Faced McDougal from a home-made one. In the country of gorge-and-puke consumption, the catch-and-release angler rejoices in his ethical apartness. And quite right, too, because if American anglers killed the trout they caught, there would soon be no trout left.

Catch-and-release, apart from its virtues in preserving the fish population, is the liar's friend: All trout grow when you let them go. Most fly fishers lie, but they do not compete. Or to put it more precisely, there are no frames within which they *can* compete. For "coarse" freshwater anglers, there are.

The fishing tournament, American style, is a wildly mutated descendant of local competitions that developed among English coarse-fishers generations ago. As trout and salmon streams were closed to the hoi polloi in the nineteenth century, other opportunities to fish appeared. The Industrial Revolution changed fishing, along with everything else in England. It brought a great increase of sport fishing among ordinary working people. An ever-expanding railway net put thousands of folk within reach of canals, ponds, and flooded quarry pits that were the by-products of industry. "Coarse" fish swam in them: pike and carp, tench and bream, and so on down to the tiny dace and gudgeon. The tackle for catching them evolved in a different direction to that of fly anglers: rods became immensely long, lines were often fixed rather than wound on a reel. Coarse-fishing clubs and societies proliferated. So did customs peculiar to the sport, such as the fishing tournament, a thing unheard of among trout fishermen but very popular at this democratic level. A strict practice of catch-and-release came to prevail. Since there was little point in distinguishing between one fish that weighed three ounces and another of three and a quarter, the prize tended to go to the biggest aggregate weight of fish—kept alive, weighed at the end of the day, and then released unharmed. No less than the fly fishers, the coarse-anglers grew acutely aware of the need for conservation, without which their sport would disappear.

The most elaborate form of this impulse today

is the freshwater bass-fishing tournament. It combines things that would have been as incomprehensible to earlier twentieth-century fishermen as to Izaak Walton: the private sport turns aggressively public, the contemplative craft becomes a competitive spectacle, an exhibition. It seems to be an iron law of American life that this always happens to sports and pastimes. Even baseball began as a long, pastoral game without showbiz overtones; as Neil Gabler reminds us in his book *Life, the Movie,* its changes were forced by "trying to survive in a twentieth-century entertainment society that prized fast, hyper and sensational. . . . The new sports of choice were football and basketball, which were better suited to the esthetics of television and to the ever-growing demand for bigger, faster, louder that was the entertainment equivalent of a new drug high." One could hardly credit that much excitement could be whipped up by the sight of folk trying to catch smallmouth bass, but one would, apparently, be wrong. It all depends on how you get to the target audience. If American know-how can put men on the moon, it can turn bassing into a spectator sport.

Bass, both largemouth *(Micropterus salmoides)* and smallmouth *(M. dolomieu)*, are God's chief gift to the American freshwater angler. They live in ponds, lakes, swamps, bayous, canals, and river deltas all over the United States and seem impervious to environmental miseries that would put most other fish out of commission. They eat voraciously, breed copiously, and fight hard for their size, which rarely goes above six pounds. They are accessible to any kid who can get near fresh water. For many Americans they are democracy with fins, up there in the national pantheon with Big Macs, Old Glory, and family values. Since they will eat anything short of a Marlboro butt, they sustain an industry of lure makers, all of them turning out creepers, poppers, Hoppy Frogs, surface plugs, wigglers, wobblers, divers, jelly worms, and other pseudocritters in iridescent or fluorescent plastic, with or without sound effects. Then there are the special bass boats, with 225-horsepower outboards to blast them across the water and silent electric motors to creep up on bass habitat; the electronic fish finders; the live wells; the trucks and trailers; and all the other trimmings. No one could deny the bass its place in the economic mainstream.

Still and all, someone else catching a bass can be a boring sight, as anyone knows who has channel-surfed into one of those cable programs featuring phlegmatic good ol' boys reeling them in. (*Close-up of small, indignant fish.* PISCATOR I: "Ah thut he wuz a pahnd bigger thun thet, the way he fought." PISCATOR II: "Yup.") So how do you turn an inherently solitary sport into an all-American spectacle like a big-league game or a rodeo?

The answer is the bass-fishing contest, whose acme is the annual BASS Masters Classic World Championship Tournament. You can't just roll up, register, and compete in it, any more than you can in the U.S. Open or at Wimbledon. Many are called, as the Good Book declares, but few are chosen. It is preceded by some twenty preliminary local fish-offs, from Lake Okeechobee in Florida to Lake Powell in Arizona. From the top-scoring fishermen in each (there are, as yet, no female pro bass anglers), forty-five win their invitations to the grand final, which is held in a different spot each year: Greensboro, North Carolina, in 1998, New Orleans in 1999. "Forty-five heroes chasing their American dream," effuses a press release from *Bassmaster*, and they're not kidding. The first prize is $100,000, plus considerable picking in endorsements from scores of sponsors—not up there with Andre Agassi's earnings yet, but not to be sneezed at, either. Last year the heroes and their fans were treated to a "pre-weigh-in extravaganza complete with laser lights and a nationally recognized singer," the country-and-western star Mark Chesnutt; and to mark the start of the Kmart Kids Classic and Autograph Day, Sergeant Tom Weigos, a member of the U.S. Golden Knights parachuting team stationed at Fort Bragg, executed a flawless parachute jump from three thousand feet, carrying the Stars and Stripes, landing smack on the rear deck of a Ranger bass boat, where he picked up a rod and made the first cast of the competition. The 1999 event promises to be even more extreme, with daily weigh-ins held in the Superdome and a nearby convention center full of hundreds of thousands of square feet of fishing equipment on display, while, in the mornings, the forty-five bass heroes advance upon the water in full parade mode, each accompanied by a journalist. "The 45 identical Ranger bass boats," declares the promo sheet,

> towed by 45 matching Chevy trucks, carry the Classic contenders to the launch ramp behind an early-morning police escort each fishing day. Spectators line the highway . . . to watch their heroes take to the

water. Amid the click and whir of cameras and the cheers of fans, the anglers try to concentrate on such things as fishing patterns, strategy, lure selection and weather.

It can't be easy, thinking about fish through all those clicks and whirs and rah-rahs, still less with a scribbling hack making notes in the boat all day. But if Tiger Woods can focus under stress, so can a Bassmaster.

III

TROUBLED WATER

FISHING IS A CRUEL SPORT. All blood sports are, though that is not necessarily a reason for abolishing them. How would you like it if fish and angler were reversed? It is a bright, breezy May day and you are strolling along one of the piers at Malibu. You stop at a vendor's cart and buy a hot dog with mustard and relish. You lean on the railing and take a first bite. Suddenly your gullet is convulsed with a choking pain and a sharp pull snaps your head forward and down. Something hard, sharp, and metallic is stuck in your throat. The shock is completely outside your experience. In an effort to resist it, you run frantically back and forth on the pier, but the pressure is inexorable, and your lungs have begun to fill with blood. Over the side you go, and hit the water wildly struggling. The unidentifiable force drags you down. On the bed of the bay, something enormous and unknown grabs you and, if you are lucky, kills you with a blow to the back of the head. If you are not so lucky, death comes more slowly by drowning. Either way, perhaps mercifully, you cannot hear or understand the Thing on the seabed chatting to its fellow Things about how well you fought.

This is more or less what happens to a hooked fish when it is pulled into a boat and left to strangle in air. At one time or another, anglers have made all manner of dumb defenses against the charge that their sport is cruel—typically, that fish don't feel pain as we do. This may or may not be true; all I can say, after fifty years of intermittent angling, is that if what they feel isn't pain, it is something so close to it as to make no difference. It may be that the hooked tarpon, with its rocklike mandibles undersupplied (by human standards) with nerves, feels no more in the course of the fight than you or I would at the dentist's. But because fish cannot communicate with us, or we with them, we do not know and never will. I have never known an angler who got pleasure from inflicting pain on a fish. Yet it defies reason to suppose that hooked fish do not suffer.

But reason is also defied by supposing that the angler, with his line and hook, is intruding into some kind of natural paradise—perhaps the octopus' garden of which the Beatles sang—where mermaids play and pain and violent death are unknown. Nothing that amateur anglers do to their prey even begins to rival in savagery what fish do to one another, or to other species. From the mayfly's point of view, the prettily speckled trout is a hellish monster. The coral polyp, if it knew dread, would dread the crunching jaws of the tropical wrasse. The bluefish loves to kill beyond the bounds of its own appetite, and will devour the young of its own species as impartially as sand eels or menhaden. And let's not get started on the dietary habits of the shark, the playful dolphin, or Willie the Killer Whale. It's Murderland down there, high tide or low, night and day. Fish have no ethics, only desires and instincts.

In any case, the urgent question is not what individual fish feel. Rather, it concerns the fate of entire species, and of the oceans in which they swim. Hook-and-line anglers have rarely had more than a marginal effect on fish populations.

High-technology commercial fishing now does. Two hundred or even a hundred years ago, fish were protected by the otherness and impenetrability of the sea. Today, they are menaced by it. The sea's fauna are strip-mined, to an extent not imaginable a few human generations ago; the fishing industry is devouring its own future. Those who oppose this find themselves up against public incomprehension, because most people can't imagine the sea as they can imagine the land. Worse, they have difficulty entertaining the idea that the sea and its contents are as essential to human life, both physical and spiritual, as the land and the air. And yet, 97 percent of our biosphere, the surface of our globe, is ocean. "Every breath we take," wrote the marine biologist Sylvia Earle, formerly the chief scientist of the National Oceanic and Atmospheric Association,

> is possible because of the life-filled, life-giving sea; oxygen is generated there, carbon dioxide absorbed . . . without the living ocean there would be no life on land . . . the sea is Earth's life-support system. The services provided are so fundamental that most of us . . . take them for

granted. In the past century, without much thought about the consequences, we have removed billions of tons of living creatures from the sea and added to it billions of tons of toxic substances. Fish, whales, shrimp, clams and other living things are regarded as commodities, not as vital components of a living system on which we are utterly dependent.

From childhood, most Americans today are pumped full of the image of Nature as a planet-sized petting zoo. Its icons are benign, warm-blooded, air-breathing, and for the most part mammalian: the dog, the cat, the rabbit, the frisky lamb, the otter, the harp seal, the koala, the lion, the bear, and the tiger (preferably when they are cubs), the panda, and winsome Bambi. Almost all of them are land-based. The only sea creatures on the list are also air-breathing, viviparous mammals: the bottle-nosed dolphin, *Tursiops truncatus,* with that built-in smile on its snoot, and of course the whales, great and small.

It is easy to have respect for creatures somewhat like ourselves. The real test is to feel it for the immense majority of species that are totally unlike us. Serious concern for Nature must begin with a recognition of its otherness. The "pathetic fallacy"— the habit of ascribing human emotions and impulses to nonhuman entities—is to conservation what a set of training wheels is to biking. It gets the kiddies going, but it has to be left behind. Otherwise, bad luck for the uncuddly, the nonfeathered, the wet, the cold-blooded, and the myriad creatures that have more than four legs or none at all.

Part of the difficulty in protecting fish, or at least in regulating and reducing their wholesale killing, is their utter unlikeness to us. They are not mammals, not warm-blooded, not air-breathing, not "intelligent" (at least, not in a way remotely perceptible to us); they are cold and dumb and slimy, though indubitably good to eat. They do not seem emotional. They do not copulate and give birth to their young. They have no conception of nurture: From the instant a fish larva is out of its egg, it's on its own among millions of others, most of which will die, not infrequently gobbled up by members of their own species. And they live in an environment that seems utterly alien to ours, the watery planet whose surface most humans never penetrate. We know less about the depths of the sea than we know about the surface of Mars or

the moon. Our love for other species is highly se-
lective, verging on a sort of mammalian narcissism.
The world's disappearing fish populations are not
going to be saved by impulses based on sentiment
or empathy, because *Homo sapiens* has no more
empathy for fish than fish do for us. When the
mad blonde played by Glenn Close in *Fatal Attrac-
tion* boiled a pet rabbit, the audience was horrified.
Few people feel a similar revulsion when a lobster,
a mud crab, or a crawfish is boiled alive. They just
reach for the mayonnaise and dig right in, as I do.
Nobody cares much about the semiferal cats that
infest the Shelter Island dump, but if I were to go
there at dawn with, say, a light spinning rod and
half a frankfurter on a #6 hook to enjoy the thrill
of playing one among the burst garbage bags and
junked TV sets until, exhausted and struggling
weakly, it submitted to the net, to be released hurt
but otherwise unharmed—in other words, if I
treated an ownerless kitty the way millions of
Americans treat the bass in their nearby ponds any
day of the week—I would certainly be viewed by
some neighbors as deeply eccentric and by others
as not far removed from the hero of *The Silence of
the Lambs*.

The fishing industry differs from all other food
industries in that it is the only one based on the

catching, killing, and processing of wild animals. On the earth or in the air, the term *game* has become all but meaningless—it refers to creatures that were once hunted wild, but are now farmed. The venison you eat was not shot in the woods; it was raised on a farm, like any ordinary steer. Likewise the quail, the pheasant, and the partridge are all raised like so many chickens, though (sometimes) with a freer range than the wretched commercial hen. The only way to eat a wild bird is to shoot it yourself, or to find one of the dwindling band of poulterers who handle them.

Some fish, too, are farmed. Between a quarter and a half of all the salmon the world eats are raised by humans. But this has done nothing to reduce the pressure on wild migratory salmon, and the growing indications are that fish farming can and does do fatal damage to its underwater environment. It takes about 3 kilograms of ground-up fish to produce 1 kilogram of living salmon. Much of this fish meal goes uneaten and joins the steady rain of fish shit on the bed of the bay, loch, or fjord where the salmon are penned. The result is pure toxicity, accompanied by algal blooms and epidemic diseases that can spread to wild salmon populations outside. For related reasons, the large-scale, high-intensity shrimp farming that is practiced on the mangrove coasts of Thailand, Cambodia, Vietnam, and parts of tropical South America has also brought ecological collapse in its train.

It is thanks to the high-tech commercial pursuit of wild fish that the population of the world's oceans is dying, with little prospect of recovery in sight. "In terms of seemliness," wrote James Hamilton-Paterson in his excellent book *The Great Deep: The Sea and Its Thresholds*, "it is no longer possible to propose fish-eating as somehow less objectionable than meat-eating. In terms of ecological damage, the worldwide plundering of marine life may turn out to have been even more disastrous than the felling of rain forest for the benefit of beef ranchers." The world population of fish-eating humans is large enough to bring whole species to the verge of extinction. Modern electronics—gadgets that are the big brothers of the fish finders and sonar units that every inshore amateur or offshore charter skipper has as a matter of course—enable fishing ships to zero in on a pod of albacore twenty miles away. They can surprise fish in the previously unreachable quarters of the ocean where they congregate to spawn. They can take out huge concentrations of sexually mature fish, on which the future of populations depends. Shallow waters are relentlessly plowed by beam trawlers, which drag heavy chains across the bottom to harry fish into their nets, thus destroying the bottom-dwelling foods (worms, clams, sea urchins) of future generations and ripping out the weed habitat. In the deep ocean, factory ships up to three hundred feet in length, with their own industrial processing and freezing plants on board, draw giant nets that can pull in tens of thousands of fish at a haul. Or the nets are even larger, and left free to float, entangling whatever comes their way. Every night for six months of the year, somewhere between fifteen hundred and two thousand ships, in aggregate the world's largest fishing fleet, are at work in the North Pacific. Each of them has laid between thirty and fifty miles of drift net, which floats freely in the ocean currents, making in aggregate a shifting, discontinuous, and impassable wall of fine nylon monofilament mesh, forty feet deep and somewhere between 45,000 and 100,000 miles in length. Practically nothing can touch this deadly web without being entangled in it: not whales or dolphins, not pelagic fish, not even sea birds. Most of the contents of the drift nets are viewed as waste and dumped overboard, where they die, if they are not dead already. This by-catch, as it is called, of industrial trawling and drift netting amounts to about a quarter of the total annual catch—27,000,000 tons of waste fish a year. Being creatures of no particular economic interest, these fish become the subjects of what military jargon in the Gulf War called "collateral damage." It is the most conscienceless and indiscriminate way of "harvesting" sea creatures—to use the fatuous euphemism preferred by the fishing industry, which would like you to suppose that the slaughters that ensue were something like the reaping of a renewable crop like wheat—that has ever been devised. But of course, humankind cannot plant new "crops" of bluefin tuna or Pacific salmon; all we can do—in the absence of sufficient internationally agreed and seriously enforceable limits on the catch—is deplete the existing populations so far that their breeding base is damaged or destroyed, which in turn leads to an even more destructive downward spiral of overfishing. Then the pressure moves to other species. Often, little is known about the nature and habits of the new target fish, with unfortunate results. One of the most popular food fishes of recent years has been a deep oceanic dweller called, for its spiny appearance, an orange roughy. Many thousands of tons had been hauled from the Pacific before, ten years into the fishery, it was discovered that orange roughies did not attain sexual maturity—and hence could not spawn—until they were thirty years old, and that the specimens of marketable size were probably closer to a hundred. Overfishing left no backup stock from which the species could regenerate.

In the worst cases, no moratorium on fishing can bring the population back. A complex and insufficiently understood web of ecological factors that had been in place for millions of years before man's impact was felt in the oceans has begun to collapse under stresses it was never designed to absorb. In 1950, according to a 1996 cover report in *Time*, the worldwide catch of oceanic fish was no more than 20 million tons a year. By 1989, it was 86 million tons, and from that peak it began to drop—the fish populations had reached their limit of exploitation, with too many high-tech fishermen chasing too few fish. That, in essence, is what happened to the once infinite-seeming cod population of the Great Banks; it happened to the fisheries of the North Sea; now it is the Pacific's turn. And the international waters of the Pacific are too big to effectively police. The Japanese, whose government has shown itself to be an entrenched enemy of all serious restrictions on worldwide industrial fishing, knew exactly what to do in the national waters around their coast. There, drift nets have been banned for years.

One single recipe can imperil a species. The southern redfish, also known as channel bass or drum, *Sciaenops ocellata,* led a fairly balanced collective life, pursued by fishermen both commercial and sporting but not under excessive pressure, until the early 1980s, when a New Orleans cook named Paul Prudhomme created a vogue for something called blackened redfish. This recipe consisted of taking a fillet of redfish, covering it on both sides with enough hot pepper and herbs to deprive it of any perceptible taste of its own, and then burning it in an iron pan over furious heat until it was encased in a black crust of carbon. This treat (inedible, to my palate, and a standing refutation of Brillat-Savarin's generally sound dictum that the discovery of a new dish brings more happiness to mankind than the discovery of a star) became so widely imitated and consumed throughout the United States that within a few years the redfish was in danger of extinction. Fortunately, restrictions were slapped on the fishery, the vogue passed, and the species seems to have weathered the threat.

Other fish have not fared so well. The case of the bluefin tuna is instructive. Sixty years ago, when the Lerners and Farringtons were chasing them for sport, practically the only part of the tuna a Nova Scotia fisherman could make money on was, strangely enough, the oil in its liver. The mass American palate developed a liking for canned tuna, but that was white-fleshed albacore, not the deep-red bluefin. Even in the late 1960s, on the northeast coast, tuna were not esteemed as a market fish. Dockside, they might reach 35 cents a pound, mostly as future pet food. But then, at the end of the 1970s, the vogue for sushi and sashimi hit American eating habits, and every yuppie from Malibu to SoHo, along with his rail-thin girlfriend, had to learn to eat raw fish, of which the most inviting (because it's red and vaguely beeflike) was the slice of *maguro*, the fillet of flesh from the upper flank of the bluefin, draped over a green dab of wasabi on its lozenge of vinegar-flavored rice. By the late eighties, tuna steaks—seared and rare, rather than cooked right through—were bidding fair to replace the proletarian burger on the summer barbecues of the Hamptons.

Of course, while the round-eyed barbarians were belatedly acquiring a taste for raw tuna, the Japanese had been fulfilling theirs since the middle Edo period. Millions upon millions of those tiny red fillets were disappearing down the collective Japanese throat every day, and to supply them—

since the offshore seas of Japan itself were effectively fished out—Japanese drift netters and long-liners were scouring the world's oceans, bringing back nearly limitless tons of *Thunnus thynnus* for home consumption. They caught them off the Atlantic coast of the United States and then they caught them in the Gulf of Mexico, where bluefin go to congregate and spawn. And from the mid-1980s on, the docks of Montauk, at the eastern tip of Long Island, were full of Japanese buyers, ready to pay unheard-of, unimagined prices, sometimes beyond $35 a pound, a hundred times their old price, for prime giant bluefin tuna in top condition. Multiplied across a five-hundred-pound fish, that was real money. And it was only the tiny visible tip of the trade, since most Atlantic tuna were and still are caught by long-liners, not sport fishermen. The big fish would go into an insulated body bag, and that night it would be on its way in the hold of a JAL jet to Tokyo, where, fresh as a daisy, it would appear in the colossal Tsukiji fish market, its better cuts of *toro*, the richly fat-marbled belly meat, auctioned by wholesaler to retailer for $100 or more a pound, ending up in the costlier restaurants at $75 for two slices the size of your index finger: the most expensive and sought-after food animal on earth. A single giant bluefin, a 715-pounder, recently was sold for $83,500 in Tsukiji. This represents a form of gastronomic fetishism that, in years to come, may seem to rival the loonier excesses of ancient Roman gastronomy, such as lark's-tongue pie—though the biomass of bluefin tuna today certainly exceeds that of Italian larks in Lucullus' day.

Nevertheless, the bluefin tuna population of the western Atlantic is collapsing, perhaps to the unsustainable level where the breeding stock, if fishing pressure continues, may never recover. This impending disaster is the result of greed, denial, political manipulation, and sheer supinity on the part of authorities and organizations whose supposed task is to protect bluefin stocks. The best account of it—and of other crises in worldwide fish population as well—comes from the marine scientist Dr. Carl Safina, who since 1990 has directed the Living Oceans Program at the National Audubon Society. His book *Song for the Blue Ocean* (1997) is the finest thing yet written on ocean conservation, a remarkable piece of reporting on fish and those who pursue them on the shores of Europe, America, and Asia, written with genuine lyrical power and underwritten by firsthand expe-

rience—Dr. Safina is a fisherman and not merely a
dry-seat scientist pushing numbers through a com-
puter. He relates how an international body set up
in the 1960s, representing some twenty Atlantic
countries and Japan, which is the largest consumer
of Atlantic tuna, managed to bury and contradict
its own findings on tuna stock. Through its own
scientists, the International Commission for the
Conservation of Atlantic Tunas (ICCAT) learned
that the breeding stock of Atlantic bluefin tuna
had declined by almost 90 percent since the mid-
1970s. They are not the only major Atlantic
species reduced to their lowest level on record.
Others include the blue and white marlin, the
swordfish, and the yellowfin, bigeye, and albacore
tunas. One would suppose this would have caused
the gravest anxiety in a conservation and management body such as ICCAT. Apparently not. ICCAT
has the power to fix catch quotas, but the only
ones it has are for bluefin tuna and swordfish. But,
Safina notes with asperity, "those quotas have always been much higher than [its own] scientists
recommended—and much higher than the populations could withstand. The commission has in
effect presided over the depletion of many of
the Atlantic's big fishes. This illustrious résumé

suggests that the acronym ICCAT might as well stand for International Conspiracy to Catch All the Tunas."

The destruction of fish populations in the deep oceans is paralleled by the appalling damage done by overfishing along coasts and reefs. The Japanese and others particularly like rich, oily fish such as tuna. In China and much of Southeast Asia, however, the preference is for white-fleshed, flaky fish, particularly the snappers, groupers, and wrasses, most of which are reef dwellers. Because the Chinese, in particular, are obsessively finicky about the absolute freshness of their seafood, these have to reach the market (and thence, the restaurant) alive, shipped in tanks from the coastal waters of the Philippines, Indonesia, New Guinea, and Micronesia. The enormous volume of the live-fish trade in the Far East relies on the irreversible destruction of their reef habitat. The fish are caught, not with hook and line, not even with nets, but with sodium cyanide, a deadly poison. Divers swim down on the coral and inject liquid cyanide (supplied by the fish market middlemen) into its holes and crevices with plastic squirt-bottles. The dazed and disoriented fish come blundering out and are easily taken, though perhaps three-quarters of them (the less commercially valuable species) will be lost on the reef. Transferred to holding pens and thence to tanks, most of the remainder will last long enough to survive the sea voyage (or, for the most valuable fish, the flight) to Hong Kong, Taiwan, Singapore, and their restaurants. Eventually they would die from the cyanide if they were not eaten first. It is something to think about the next time you are in a Chinese restaurant with its aquarium tanks full of fish. Sometimes the fishers—dirt-poor sea peasants, struggling to survive in an inexorably declining fishery—also die from cyanide poisoning. And the reefs, too, perish. Cyanide is supertoxic to coral. Parrotfish eat weed, thus cleaning the coral surface; as their population declines, the coral smothers and dies. Thus the ravenous appetite for reef fish destroys the habitat in which future generations of fish might breed, and the melancholy history of destruction that has been visited on terrestrial species is repeated in the sea. Marine scientists estimate that 90 percent of the 34,000 square kilometers of coral reef around the Philippine archipelago is dying or already dead from a combination of cyanide fishing, weed overgrowth, industrial pollution, and soil runoff from deforested coast. "An active cyanide user," Carl Safina reports, doses fifty coral heads a day, about 225 days a year. In the Philippines alone, some three thousand cyanide users squirt tens of millions of coral heads each year. At this point, just stopping cyanide fishing would be a victory. Never mind catch limits. Never mind quota restrictions. An unrestricted hook-and-line fishery—what we consider uncontrolled, unmanaged fishing in the West—would seem a blessing in the Indo-Pacific, compared to what's now happening here.

Does the sport fisherman, the recreational angler, feel responsible for this situation? Obviously not. Yet both the angler and the industrial fleet share the same oceans and, inevitably, the same fate. There are some kinds of sport fishing that now seem unacceptable, at least to me. In part this is a private matter: I am sixty, and as one gets older one views all death with less indifference.

That of a marlin, for instance. Marlin are among the most beautiful creatures in the world, even when they are dead and their colors have gone. But live, in all their power and iridescence, light and water flowing from their bodies, silver and lavender, no words can do them justice: It's like trying to describe an archangel with fins, not wings. When they walk on their tails across the water, or start a plunging run to the horizon, blazing silver amid the white foam, with the line training behind in a long catenary, you feel awe at the sight and privilege at being one of the (relatively) few people to see such a thing. But what is this talk of "privilege" when the fish is going to die, after hours of torment, with a razor-barbed #12/0 hook embedded in its gullet or gills? I have never caught a really large billfish, and now if I were offered the chance to do so, I would not take it. The bigger the fish, the less likely it is to survive the ordeal, and the rarer these creatures get, the hollower the desire to catch them becomes. The broadbill swordfish is facing extinction and should be left alone. Marlin taste delicious, and nothing can save them from the Japanese, Taiwanese, and Korean long-liners, who inflict an immense carnage upon them, grinding them up to make millions of pounds of fish sausage and fish paste, *surimi*, a year. But one wonders if, from the fish's point of view, there was ever much difference between dying ignominiously on a long line and dying, nobly we are told, on a shorter line connected to Ernest Hemingway, Zane Grey, or oneself. The pursuit of big-game records, which inspired the Hemingways and Glassells of another generation, now seems a peculiarly empty form of machismo, however intense the momentary triumph, however mingled its impulses may be with estheticism. (Nevertheless, I am fairly sure that big-game fishing obsessed Hemingway not because he was a killer, but because he was an esthete, a stylist.) Big-game fishermen, who need to be rich to fish consistently, now spend vast amounts of money chasing what is considered to be the holy grail of such fishing, two-thousand-pound black marlin, which have been seen but not caught in the Pacific Ocean off Queensland in Australia. And when one is finally caught, what happens? A statistic is added to the IGFA records; a ton of living wildness is subtracted, forever, from nature. It seems an obscenely uneven trade-off. And the photographs from the second third of the twentieth century of big-game champions on the dock beside their huge dead prey seem, increasingly, to belong as much to another world as the nineteenth-century photographs of Indian rajahs and their guest sahibs, or African white hunters and their clients, posed with the Bengal tigers and black rhinos they wantonly shot.

I don't want to catch shark, either. In the early 1950s the idea that sharks were anything but an enemy would have been regarded by most Australians, and Americans, too, as insane. And yet, statistically, they posed far less threat to human life than did crossing a suburban street. The idea that shark fishermen made the water safer for swimmers was the merest flummery, without a jot of evidence to back it up. You might as well defend elephant or lion killing in Africa on the grounds that the death of these magnificent quadrupeds makes it safer for people to wander as they please on the veldt. So it might—very marginally. But what of it? After Steven Spielberg's *Jaws*, that witless knockoff of *Moby-Dick*, became a smash hit, Americans went into prolonged shark shock. They were happy that after years of listening to conservationists' lectures on the sanctity of Nature, Hollywood had given them something natural to hate—*Carcharodon carcharias,* the great white, twenty feet of insatiable appetite and rampant id, the mother of all otherness. Armies of middle-aged dentists from New Jersey, bursting with testosterone, sallied forth to Montauk to hire boats and prove what tough guys they were by hauling in a shark, any shark, though preferably a great white. Charter captains, notably Frank Mundus, supposedly the Ahab figure on whom the obsessed shark-chaser of *Jaws* was modeled, made their retirement money off this reverse feeding frenzy. No catch-and-release here: You can't release a gut-hooked shark, you have to kill it. And then, for want of anything better to do with its carcass, string it up and have your photo taken with it before it goes in the fish-meal grinder. As a sporting spectacle, it had all the allure of watching dogs being bludgeoned to death in a pool.

Nor was it rendered any more edifying by the thought of the wholesale slaughter of sharks on the other side of the world—by Southeast Asian and Japanese long-liners, for instance, who haul in countless thousands of sharks every week, hack off their fins to be dried for Chinese soup, and dump the still-living, helpless bodies back in the ocean. Big sharks have few defenders, but now they need all they can get, though they don't know it. At least the Australian government has declared the great white a protected species, along with the saltwater crocodile, the largest and most dangerous reptile on earth, which until 1971 was being shot to extinction. That is as it should be, for we have no moral right to preserve only cuddly tourist attractions like the koala. Wildness, otherness, and dread, embodied in living creatures, also have their claims. It is beneficial, if you find yourself casting a fly for barramundi from a small aluminum skiff in the waters of a north Australian coastal billabong, to see a saltie longer than the boat swim by. It puts you in your place. For that, it is worth losing the occasional careless tourist.

Take the fear and trembling out of nature and you're left with Disney World. The "watery part of the world," as Herman Melville called it, is a zone of fear and trembling, as well as a place of endless curiosity, fascination, and delight. The waters teach us that we are not the lords of the universe, with all other living creatures our vassals and serfs. The Genesis account of creation—God setting man in dominion over the earth and all its creatures—has become one of the most destructive myths ever to encumber the human mind. We are part of a chain of being, or rather a vastly intricate net, whose integrity we violate to our own peril as individuals and as a species. It is a lesson driven home repeatedly by conservationists on land, but although it applies just as forcibly to the sea its application there is less understood. We need to understand it. Angling, at its best, is a means to that understanding.

There is no defensible ethic or esthetic of angling that doesn't center on moderation. Just as a properly trained hunter should never point his gun, let alone fire a shot, at a living animal that he doesn't intend to eat, so an angler should never kill a fish that will not reach the table in a state of perfect freshness. The others can be released. Which means that you should always stop—stop killing, not necessarily fishing—when you have enough on the beach or in the live well to feed you and yours for the next day or two. This does not diminish the pleasure of the sport. Rather, it enhances it. Who really needs all that dead seafood? Just as there is one moment in the life of a peach when it is perfectly ripe, so the special pleasure of eating fish arises when you have caught the creature yourself and it is just out of the water. Offering your friends a poached striped bass that you caught yesterday evening is qualitatively different from feeding them one you bought in a shop. No flatfish ever tasted as good to me as the flounder I would fillet on board a friend's ancient rust bucket in the Peconic Bays, wrap in aluminum foil with a pinch of salt and pepper, and cook on the engine manifold. Of all the sashimi I have eaten over the years, the best was on Alan Shields's boat off Montauk, when, having brought wasabi, soy sauce, and my second-best *deba-bocho* (sushi knife) along, I would take a thin slice or two off the flank of a just-caught yellowfin tuna and, having admired the rainbow glimmer of transected fibers in the flesh (like a diffraction grating), gobble it down for breakfast. I may sound like a fanatic, but I disapprove of home-freezing surplus fish. The end product can't be distinguished from what you can buy in a market, so why bother?

A sense of moderation invites you to scale down your tackle, to accept the gratification of medium success with more demanding techniques in place of a big bag: lighter lines, thinner rods, saltwater flies instead of live baits or spun lures. Nobody really respects a meat fisherman, except other meat fishermen. Official record sizes don't matter anymore—not, at least, to the fishers I know. It is better to release a fish than to keep it, even when minimum-size rules permit you to keep. A rhyme from my childhood, read in some fishing anthology, sticks in my head:

> Enjoy the stream, thou harmless Fish!
> And when the angler, for his dish,
>   Through Gluttony's vile sin,
> Attempts (the wretch) to pull thee out,
> God give thee strength, thou gentle Trout,
>   To pull the Rascal in.

I don't know that I'd quite endorse that—I am too gluttonous to do so without hypocrisy—but one gets the point. The joy of fishing is in the catching, not the killing; and, much of the time, in the not-catching as well, the absorption in Nature. Anglers see only a tiny corner of the vast life of the world's waters. But what they do see, they are apt to see thoroughly. Walton and his successors were right about that. Sometimes the empty cooler contains the finest sashimi.

Index

A Note on The Library of Contemporary Thought

This exciting new series tackles today's most provocative, fascinating, and relevant issues, giving top opinion makers a forum to explore topics that matter urgently to themselves and their readers. Some will be think pieces. Some will be research oriented. Some will be journalistic in nature. The form is wide open, but the aim is the same: to say things that need saying.

Now available from
**THE LIBRARY OF CONTEMPORARY
THOUGHT**

VINCENT BUGLIOSI
NO ISLAND OF SANITY
Paula Jones v. Bill Clinton
The Supreme Court
on Trial

JOHN FEINSTEIN
THE FIRST COMING
Tiger Woods:
Master or Martyr?

PETE HAMILL
NEWS IS A VERB
Journalism at the End of the
Twentieth Century

CARL HIAASEN
TEAM RODENT
How Disney Devours
the World

SEYMOUR M. HERSH
AGAINST ALL ENEMIES
Gulf War Syndrome: The
War Between America's
Ailing Veterans and Their
Government

**EDWIN
SCHLOSSBERG**
INTERACTIVE
EXCELLENCE
Defining and Developing
New Standards
for the Twenty-first Century

ANNA QUINDLEN
HOW READING
CHANGED MY LIFE

**WILLIAM STERLING
AND STEPHEN WAITE**
BOOMERNOMICS
The Future of Your
Money in the Upcoming
Generational Warfare

JIMMY CARTER
THE VIRTUES
OF AGING

SUSAN ISAACS
BRAVE DAMES AND
WIMPETTES
What Women Are Really
Doing on Page and Screen

HARRY SHEARER
IT'S THE STUPIDITY,
STUPID
Why (Some) People Hate
Clinton and Why the Rest
of Us Have to Watch

STEPHEN JAY GOULD
ROCKS OF AGES
Science and Religion in the
Fullness of Life

JONATHAN KELLERMAN
SAVAGE SPAWN
Reflections on Violent Children

Look for this title coming soon from
The Library of Contemporary Thought

WALTER MOSLEY
WORKIN' ON THE CHAIN GANG
Shaking Off the Dead Hand of History